NOBODY'S CHILD:
How Older Women Say Good-bye to Their Mothers

Diane Sher Lutovich

Baywood Publishing Company, Inc.
AMITYVILLE, NEW YORK

Library of Congress Catalog Number: 00-045530
ISBN: 0-89503-253-8 (paper)

Library of Congress Cataloging-in-Publication Data

Lutovich, Diane, 1937–
    Nobody's child : how older women say good-bye to their mothers / Diane Lutovich.
        p. cm.
    Includes bibliographical references and index.
    ISBN 0-89503-253-8 (paper)
        1. Grief. 2. Bereavement- -Psychological aspects. 3. Loss (Psychology) 4.
    Mothers--Death--Psychological aspects. 5. Mothers and daughters--Psychology. I. Title.

BF575.G7 L88 2000
155.9'37--dc21
                                                            00-045530

Acknowledgments

I want to pay special tribute to all the women who spoke so openly to me about a very special part of their lives. They shared willingly and freely and did so not only to get perspective on the meaning of their mother's death in their own lives, but to pass on something they learned that might help others. I felt connected to all of them by sharing their hurts, their joys, and their fears. Each woman was exceptional and I would love to list all of their names, but I have respected their desire for privacy and so they will be anonymous. In a way, they represent themselves and all others, as well.

I must, of course, thank my mother. Because of what she did for me and gave to me, I was able to recognize the importance of our relationship. I tried to guard her secrets, too, so just in case she were to come back, she would not feel that I "aired our dirty laundry in public."

Then I must thank Dr. Morgan who believed the book had potential; Barbara Swift Brauer, who was willing to work with my incoherent ramblings and help me bring order to them; and close friends who were kind enough to read the book and tell me how important they thought it was. My special friend David Madway deserves many thanks for believing this project had merit. Finally, my daughter, Natasha, for teaching me what mother-daughter relationships are all about from the other side of the equation, and her husband, my dear son-in-law, Greg, who has helped us look at family in a new way.

Table of Contents

Introduction

My mother died without telling me what to wear to her funeral. Looking around at how formally everyone else was dressed, I was reminded of how much I still needed her.

As deaths go, my mother's was easy, and, compared to some daughters' experiences, it was easy for me, too. She had very little anxiety, little pain that couldn't be controlled, little time to dwell on the inevitable, and just enough time to say good-bye.

I, however, wasn't ready. I wasn't ready when I had my tonsils out, I wasn't ready when my daughter was born, and I wasn't ready to be without a mother. I needed more time; I would still be the perfect daughter, the one to take her hand, bring her gifts, not scold her for keeping her rooms so hot or the television so loud. I would tell her over and over again she had been a terrific mother. Then there were the questions that I had put off—some big, some small. When was Uncle Harry's birthday? Do I beat the whites or yolks first when making her special cake—or does it matter? Am I forgiven for leaving her alone in her new widowhood so many years ago? And did she still think (as she had once joked) that the herring served at her memorial should be in sour cream?

When she died, my mother was four months short of her ninety-second birthday and I, her only daughter, was fifty-seven. Four and a half years and many losses later, I still think of her several times a day and continue to be surprised at the intensity of my feelings. I hadn't thought we had been that close. We had lived in different cities for over thirty years. We had almost never had an intimate conversation. Yet the fact remained that I wasn't ready to let her go.

1

My mother might be finished with me, but I was not finished with her, with our relationship, its issues, or its lessons.

My situation was not unique. At the time my mother died, I knew many women my age who had recently buried their mothers or knew they would be doing so soon. It must have been at least a bit of a wrench to all of them, yet none of them really talked about it. I knew every nuance of my friends' feelings about an adulterous affair, an abortion, their son's wife, their concern about hormone supplements. We dissected everything together—except our mothers' deaths. We seemed to talk all around these holes where our mothers had been (and shadows remained), but we didn't talk about the loss we felt or its meaning in our lives. Instead, a mother's death was usually announced casually, "My mother died last week." Someone would respond, "Oh, I'm so sorry; I hope she didn't suffer." And that was that. When I asked a friend why this was, she said she thought it had to do with the fact that it seemed so ordinary each woman assumed that no one would find the subject interesting enough to talk about.

I wanted to talk about it, about my own mother's death and the reaction of other women to their mothers' death. I wanted especially to hear from women like myself, whose own lives are more than half over, their children grown (or just about), who are getting ready for their own retirement. In hearing their stories, I thought I would learn more about myself and my mother, and what it means to be a woman facing the time in her life when losses begin to outnumber the gains, and she begins to plug her own numbers into the actuarial tables. I wanted to hear the little stories—what daughters did with the items they inherited and didn't want—and the big stories—like the ways they found to give themselves what their mothers would no longer give and perhaps had never been able to give them. So as a way of getting closure on my mother's life and death, I set out to discover how other women respond to the deaths of their mothers; how each adjusted to the loss of the one person who had known her longer than any other.

I had no trouble finding women to interview. I started with a few close friends and colleagues, and from there I went to women I had grown up with. I started receiving notes and calls from women hearing about my project who wanted to be interviewed, who wanted the chance to talk without interruption about their mothers and their experience of their deaths. During the interviews, the women sat with their boxes of tissue at their side and brought out pictures of their mothers or themselves as little girls with their mothers. They wanted to acknowledge they had lost something momentous—even those who were not so sorry to see their mothers die.

Women know a mother's death is a significant event, a major transition, a passage in life. Talking about it with me seemed a way they could attempt to integrate the past and the present into the future. It appeared to have something to do with fitting this one death into a larger context—the death of all mothers. They appreciated the opportunity to have someone listen while they worked through the meaning of their mothers' lives and deaths. If, at the outset, I had had some misgivings about the value of this information, each time a woman at the end of the interview stopped to thank me, to tell me how much she appreciated the opportunity to talk about her mother and her mother's death, I knew for certain that this was an important issue not only for myself but many others as well.

In all, I interviewed forty-five women, ranging in age from forty-two to seventy-one; the majority, 80 percent, were between fifty and sixty-eight. Their mothers at time of death were between seventy and ninety-seven, the majority between the ages of eighty and ninety. More than 70 percent of the mothers were widows, some for more than forty years. Many daughters stated their mothers had no religious affiliation, but of those who did, fifteen were said to be Jewish, one Buddhist, one Quaker, three Irish Catholic, and twenty-two Protestant, which included Episcopalian, Southern Baptist, and Methodist. The women I spoke with were from all parts of the United States—New York, California, Texas, Minnesota, and various points in between. The most recent death had occurred two weeks before the interview; the most distant was ten years.

None of these variables, not religion, geographical location, nor the time since death, seemed to be critical factors in how the daughters spoke about their mothers or experienced their deaths. In other words, I can't say that the difference between one woman's reactions to her mother's death only a month before and another's reaction to her mother's death seven years earlier, can be directly attributed to the amount of time that had elapsed.

Some were so locked in grief, so overcome with their loss, they could hardly get on with their lives. One woman in particular was still grief-stricken seven years later. She cried at the mention of her mother's name and had devoted a room in her home to housing her mother's things—a shrine, as it were. I learned about another woman who couldn't wait for her mother to die; she was convinced that her life would be fine if only her mother were dead and she was finally freed from trying to please her.

In undertaking this project initially, I wanted to discover the answers to many questions. I was curious to know what caused some women to literally fall apart when their mother died, others to feel a great sense of freedom, and still others to face the death with love and sadness, and move on. I wanted to learn what made the loss harder for some women than others. How long did it hurt? How do most women accommodate the loss? In its wake, are they liable to be more or less frightened at the prospect of their own deaths? Did it change their relationships to their mates, children, or other family members? I even thought I could find some important variables. Maybe I'd discover what kind of relationships were easier to let go. Maybe I'd find that those who had the most unresolved relationships with their mothers suffered less—or suffered more. I wanted equations.

But the deeper I went, the more complex the questions that surfaced: What does a daughter grieve for when her mother dies? If she doesn't feel distraught, is she a bad daughter? Does the intensity of an individual's grief correlate with other characteristics—the kind of relationship she and her mother had? The kind of mothering she received? The kind of daughter she perceived herself to be? How much did other kinds of loss limit or exacerbate feelings about the loss of a mother? Why did some daughters who took such good care of their mothers feel so much guilt after their deaths while others who did so little for their mothers never mention guilt? Was there any correlation between mothers who had fully lived their own lives and what their daughters felt at their deaths?

In the course of the interviews I found some answers, many questions, and, most definitely, a reaffirmation of the power of the mother-daughter bond. The insights I gained made me want to proceed with this book. I hope by sharing what I learned and the stories of those I talked with that this book will serve as a guide for middle-aged women affected by their mothers' death, past, present, or future. I want to offer daughters the opportunity to learn that, whatever their personal reactions, others have experienced similar feelings. It may be important for them to hear how some daughters were able to help their mothers in their final days, or how fortunate some felt to have come to terms with their mothers before they died. It gives readers an opportunity to hear from women who feel guilty whenever they think of their mothers (with or without ostensible reason), and how some of them have overcome that guilt.

I feel I even learned some things that will help make my own death easier for my daughter. I remember that a year or two before my mother died, my daughter asked me, "Do you think you'll fall apart when grandma dies?" I told her it was hard to know, but I doubted it; that was not my way. But I understood. She was worried about herself as well. I want this book for her, too, to show her there is no one way to respond to the loss of a mother. Mothers die and their daughters live.

SIGNIFICANCE OF LOSS

Until recently, researchers' interest in the reactions of middle-aged children to the death of their parents ranked far below concern for the survival of the endangered salamander. First of all, it wasn't so long ago that most parents died before their children had reached middle-age, so this is a relatively new phenomenon. According to Sidney Moss, there are other valid reasons as well. For instance, the death of an elderly parent lacks the impact of the death of a mate, child, or a younger parent; after all, the elderly are expected to die. Another factor may be that the death of an individual parent is such a solitary experience, unlike death from wars, natural disasters, and so on. And though it can hurt like hell, it is rarely a tragedy. Moss goes on to consider another reason why so little research has been done in this area:

> Even cross-cultural studies of death and dying pay scant attention to the adult child's loss of parent. Findings suggest that an adult losing a parent does not exhibit intense grief and aggression, and rarely necessitates the formal treatment which is normally given to persons in deep mourning. . . . *On the other hand, the loss of parents may be so painful that we as researchers and clinicians flee from it to protect ourselves, to escape facing our unresolved guilts and frustrations. The child in each of us may feel abandoned in losing a parent, and we shy away from the topic* (emphasis added) [1, p. 104].

From my own investigation, I would add that the responses of adult daughters to the deaths of their mothers tend to be very individualized, reflecting the unique nature of the mother-daughter relationship over a lifetime, combined with the pressures of the daughters' present circumstances. This may be true for Jasmine, whose inconsolable grief seemed to have much to do with the fact that she had always wanted her mother to admire her. Once her mother died, she had no more chances to prove her worth. Millie, on the other hand, was still adjusting to the loss of her husband, and so she had little emotion to spare for her mother's death.

Because, as Moss points out, the elderly are expected to die, the adult child is often assumed to be minimally affected. The possibility of overpowering grief is downplayed, as if it were not quite appropriate. So, while the loss may be deeply felt, society indicates over and over again that it does not accept or support profound or extended mourning in this situation [2, p. 109].

This attitude on society's part may force the daughter into the position of outwardly denying the impact of her loss despite her intense grief. Psychologists, including Anne Rosberger, conclude that losing a parent can be an extremely traumatic experience. It doesn't seem to matter how old the surviving child, that child still feels lost and alone, even abandoned [2, p. 21]. Other investigators have commented on the fact that the loss of a parent can seriously affect the adult child's mental and psychological development. Little wonder, then, that Madeline, a week after her mother died, found herself dropping things, walking into doors, and functioning poorly in other ways. Helena, who had such a close relationship with her mother and shared her mother's death so fully, came home after the death and woke up to an acute case of shingles.

Of course a daughter's loss of her elderly mother is significant. For as many as seven decades this connection has existed and, with it, all the shared memories, bad as well as good ones. Yet while a daughter might be overwhelmed with her emotions, stating, "I lost my best cheerleader," "I lost my history," "I lost my last chance at unconditional love," the world is saying to her, "Your mother lived a long life. Be grateful." "She is lucky to have died peacefully." "You were fortunate to have had her for so long." Jorrie told me these expressions just made her angry at others' insensitivity. "I didn't feel she was lucky or that I was fortunate."

For those daughters providing care for their elderly mothers, this lack of understanding presents a further paradox: at the same time she must open herself up emotionally to provide comfort and support to a failing parent, she is expected to do so with some detachment, as if society were telling her to feel enough to do a good job, but not to feel too much. (Admittedly, not so different from mothering.) When even her mother takes her efforts for granted, the daughter may feel totally abandoned (more about this in Chapter 4). One of the reasons, no doubt, the women were so happy to talk to me was that they knew that I, even though a stranger in most cases, would not disparage the meaningfulness of their loss.

As recently as the late 1980s, professional resources for these daughters dealing with their grief were hard to find. In one case, several women whose mothers had died about the same time, searched in vain for a support group, a place to share their experiences in order to reassure themselves that they were not "crazy" for feeling so bereft. Finally, in desperation, the women hired a social worker and formed their own group. Jorrie said that as soon as she heard what other women were feeling, she could see her reactions were reasonable, and she was better able to accept and work through her grief.

Today this situation is starting to change; listings in the local weekly paper reveal as many as five support or therapy groups dealing with the loss of parents, particularly mothers. One social worker holds a special workshop the day before Mother's Day for daughters whose mothers have died.

So although compassion and sympathy are still lagging, it appears that more people are beginning to recognize and express interest in this topic, and to be more willing to listen to daughters' stories, perhaps because the feelings of women in general are starting to be taken more seriously. Similarly, an increased emphasis on object relations and family therapy has psychologists looking at relationships of all sorts. Finally, the increasing number of middle-aged women (approximately 25 million between the ages of 45 and 65 according to the U.S. Department of Health and Human Services, 1996) potentially sharing this experience makes it more visible. Thus, for many of us who live in these relatively secure times, we have the opportunity to turn our attention to an important phenomenon that is increasing along with life expectancy.

Within this context, it makes sense to focus on the impact on the middle-aged daughter when her mother dies. Though male children are also affected by the loss of their mothers and both genders are affected by the death of their father, the reaction, most often, is strongest when a daughter loses her mother for all of the reasons mentioned.

MY STORY

In many ways, my own story is a reflection of what I heard from the women I interviewed. It didn't seem to matter that we all had had different relationships with our mothers, different life experiences, or different emotional makeups. What we had in common was a mother who lived long enough to be at our side through most of our major life events and allowed us to see, close-up, where we, too, are heading. We also shared what I term the "great divide," the incalculable schism between the eras of our mothers' childhoods and our own. Most of our mothers were born before World War I, grew up in a restricted, patriarchal society where women enjoyed fewer opportunities, and were seen as less capable than men; they were taught that talking about personal feelings and expressing themselves physically were as scandalous as promiscuous sex. We daughters, by contrast, went through the turbulent and liberating 1960s, bemoaning the fact that we never really knew our mothers because we never had had a real conversation with them; that our mothers were superficial, had no respect for other women and therefore could not take us seriously; that physical contact, at least by the time we were teenagers, was awkward and unnatural. And not knowing how to close this gap, we berated ourselves for not reaching across and helping our mothers into the latter part of the twentieth century—or meeting them squarely where they were. What a waste!

My relationship with my mother seems to typify most of these time-based differences. My mother was born in 1902, I in 1937. For starters, she never left the house without wearing a girdle; I threw mine away as soon as I left home. We started our relationship as two people who might have had everything in common and evolved into slightly different species. But we loved each other and we tried to be kind.

As a small child, I adored and clung to my mother. I thought she was the most beautiful, wonderful woman alive. Even though I started acting up as a teenager, my attachment didn't waver and in many ways I was still excessively dependent on her help and support. By the time my father died when I was seventeen, however, I was ready to leave home, to enter the larger world; unfortunately, it was just at the time my mother needed me. When I finished college and moved over 2,000 miles away, her need to have me at home and my need to be far away had become irreconcilable, even though we never once mentioned the fact in conversation.

After that, our relationship settled into something that was polite and superficial. Although nothing was said, I could sense that she had never forgiven me for leaving her to start my own life in a new city in a new part of the country. We were very careful to avoid subjects that could possibly upset the other. For the most part, we had stopped giving advice, showing anger or disappointment. We became more and more distant. When I was getting a divorce, I didn't tell her until after I had already moved.

Even my daughter noticed the casual superficiality of our relationship. Once, overhearing my end of a long-distance talk with my mother in which I described the weather and what I was having for lunch, she whispered, "We're never going to have such empty conversations."

Despite this relative estrangement, my mother and I were deeply attached to one another, and it should have been no real surprise that I was her choice of last resort. Years before when her aunt was dying, slowly and painfully, my mother asked me to promise to deliver the "fatal dose" when her own time came. I tried to reason with her: I argued, "You could change your mind after the fact . . . You know I'll do it wrong . . . I might do it too early." But she was unconvinced. "Who else can I ask? I could never ask your brother." (To this day, I'm sorry I didn't ask why.) Finally I said, "You're right, Mom, what's a daughter for if not to come home and kill her mother?" At that we both howled with laughter. After she returned home, she sent me a letter telling me how she wanted to die—that is, with no "heroic measures"—and I sent her a letter promising I would never let her suffer. She thanked me for my letter, saying it relieved her of a lot of anxiety, and we never mentioned it again. We didn't need to.

In 1991, a series of events convinced her she needed to move closer to me. My brother had retired and planned to live year-round in Arizona; my mother fell and broke her wrist, and she had a major falling out with my niece, the only close relative living nearby. She realized that the retirement community she had moved into four years earlier had been a bad choice; most of the people there were too old and infirm, and so she had gradually isolated herself, not even joining others for meals. And if all these were not reason enough, she was diagnosed with bladder cancer (though doctors told her that at her age the tumors would grow so slowly, she would probably die from other causes). She was frightened. She didn't want to be alone.

One day, my daughter, studying in Italy, called to tell me that she had just received two cards in one week from her grandmother, that her grandma was obviously very lonely, and I should do something about it. Since I had come to terms with the fact that my mother and I would never live in the same city, I was so taken aback that I asked "Which grandma?" although her paternal grandmother had died six years before. Either my daughter was more ready than I to hear what her grandma needed, or my mother was able to communicate to her granddaughter in a way she couldn't to me.

So despite the fact that in my adult life there had been some distance, even occasional coldness, I couldn't imagine not asking my mother to move near me. Presented with the need, I didn't waver for a second in making that call. In hindsight, I can see how much lay behind that decision. For one thing, I had never stopped trying to be the "good daughter," at least as far as I was capable; whatever I had been taught as a child had been waiting in the wings for just such a moment. I knew she had done her best to be a "good mother" to me and I was grateful. As a parent myself, I had a responsibility to my own daughter, who loved her grandmother and who was counting on me to do the right thing. I felt in some way I needed to make that call as much for my daughter's image of me as for my mother. But I also needed to do it for myself. My own conscience and the way I wanted to see myself—as a kind and caring person—left me no choice. I loved my mother and wanted to be able to "give back" to her.

So although I didn't truly believe my mother would ever want to move away from the city she had called home for almost forty years, I called her and said, "I think it is time you move out here." She was clearly far more ready than I could have guessed. She told me that I was right and that she would come in the fall. That spring, she came to look at a few residential places and chose the one near me, the one she had rejected twelve years earlier. Then she went home and packed up, said good-bye to her friends, her only living brother and a sister-in-law, people she knew she would never see again, and flew back out to California. So sure she was making the right and only decision, this ninety-year-old woman insisted we stop at the bank so she could open her checking account even before she checked into her new apartment.

Once she came to live in California, my mother and I tried desperately to be kind to one another. We were stuck together and had no choice but to learn to accommodate. After so many years it took a while to learn what the other found intrusive, irritating, overbearing. We did end up having some delicious moments in those few years before she died. We made meals together; I had parties for her. We went to concerts, saw the most magnificent production of *Swan Lake*, and I called her every day before her lunch. We didn't have much in common; she found subjects dealing with her life or mine, talk of mistakes or regrets or disappointments too painful, but we managed. Once when I had come for dinner and she was walking me to my car later in the evening, under a night bursting with stars, I asked her if she had any regrets about her move. "None," she said. "I knew it was the right thing and it was."

I certainly no longer felt I had to fight her for my independence and she was too old and too grateful to be critical of the way I lived my life or kept house. In fact, according to my friends, she even mentioned that she was proud of me. In addition to our daily calls, I saw her at least twice a week and she settled into a routine. She became very involved in her community, and spent her time between classes, lectures, friends, and discussion groups. She came alive in a way I hadn't seen since long before my father died.

More than a year passed like this and I just assumed that things would continue in the same way perhaps forever. I was in no way thinking about her death, even when she began to seem less well, more tired, and withdrawn. She began to stay in her room more and to walk with a cane. But the mother of my childhood had always been a fragile, easily tired, and withdrawn woman, so I didn't even think about what it could mean.

When her situation changed more dramatically, I still saw nothing ominous in what were obvious signs that something was terribly wrong. In fact, a few weeks before she died, when asked by one of her fellow residents how she was doing, and my mother replied, "It's not good," I chalked it up to some plea for sympathy. Cold and heartless? Maybe. Full of denial? Absolutely. Whatever time it was, it was not time for my mother to die.

How many of us have the same feelings Simone de Beauvoir described in her book, *A Very Easy Death:* "My mother had always been there, and I had never seriously thought that some day I should see her go. Her death, like her birth, had its place in some legendary time. When I said to myself, 'She is of an age to die,' the words were devoid of meaning . . ." [3, p. 20].

And then came my shock. My mother was taken to the emergency room with kidney blockage. She and her doctor agreed there would be no "heroic measures," so there were no decisions to be made and nothing to be done. It seemed so sudden to me, out of nowhere. When I got to the hospital, she was on her way to her room to die. She said just enough: "It's been a long life and a good life. I'm ready to go." And then pointing to me, she said to my friend who had accompanied me, "Isn't she beautiful?"

It was the first such compliment she had ever paid me. She had always been afraid I would be conceited, and, too, she had no experience in receiving compliments from her own mother; most painful of all, she really felt her opinions didn't count. But all of her reservations seemed to fall away with those last words. I was stunned by her strength, her beauty, and her courage.

Three days later she was dead. During that time, much of which she was in a coma, I held her hand, massaged her feet, and thought of the wonderful poem Linda Pastan had written when her mother was dying:

DUET FOR ONE VOICE

1

I sit at your side
watching the tides of consciousness
move in and out, watching
the nurses, their caps
like so many white gulls circling
the bed. The window
grows slowly dark,
and light again,
and dark. The clock
tells the same old stories.
Last week you said, now
you'll have to learn
to sew for yourself.
If the thread is boredom,

the needle is grief.
I sit here learning.

2
In place of spring
I offer this branch
of forsythia
whose yellow blossoms
I have forced.
Your tired mouth
forces a smile
in thanks. Outside
it is still cold;
who knows how long
the cold will last?
but underground,
their banners still furled,
whole armies of flowers wait.

3
I am waiting for you to die,
even as I try to coax you
back to life
with custards and soup
and colored pills I shake
from the bottle like dice,
though their magic
went out of the world
with my surgeon father,
the last magician.
I am waiting
for you to be again
what you always were,
for you to be there whole
for me to run to with this new grief—
your death—the hair grown back
on your skull the way it used to be,
your widow's peak the one sure landmark
on the map of my childhood,
those years when I believed
that medicine and love and being good
could save us all.

4
We escape from our mothers
again and again, young
Houdinis, playing the usual matinees.
First comes escape down
the birth canal, our newly carved faces
leading the way like figureheads
on ancient slaveships,
our small hands rowing for life.
Later escape into silence, escape
behind slammed door,
the flight into marriage.
I thought I was finally old enough
to sit with you, sharing a book.
But when I look up
from the page, you
have escaped from me.

Linda Pastan (Originally published in *A Fraction of Darkness,* by Linda Pastan. © 1985 by Linda Pastan. Used by permission of W.W. Norton & Company, Inc.)

My mother did not suffer long. The night before she died, she was in a deep and final coma, but the breaths kept coming. Even her nurse was baffled, but suggested that though my mother was ready to die, her space in heaven must need a little more work. I took this as a chance to tell my mother how much I loved her and reassure her that she had been a good mother. I told her it was OK to go. Her work was done.

The next morning, when I got to the hospital, the doctor told me she had just "slipped away," a few minutes earlier. "Slipped away," as if she were a cat burglar making an escape. Gone, just like that.

So many feelings flooded in, I couldn't focus on any special one. I felt lost, abandoned, lonely, shaky, full of guilt for all I'd never done or said, and, at the same time, profoundly happy for her. She had often said that she never expected to live so long, but since she had, she had one wish and that was to die quickly, with all her "marbles" intact. She got her wish. She did it in her own way, as she had done everything else in her life (at least since my father died). She had made it easy for me, just as she had always done when she had the chance. If she had not been the role model I would have chosen in life, she was and continues to be my role model for dying.

From the hospital, I went to her apartment. Everything was just
the way she left it when she went to the emergency room three days
before. It looked as if she would be returning to straighten up any
minute. Her bed was unmade. Her glasses were there, plants needing
water, some mending in a pile. I thought you should be able to make
your bed and put everything in its place before you died, especially if
you're the kind of person who has done so every day of your life.

My brother, his wife, and my daughter helped with the funeral
arrangements and announcements. At the funeral, held in
Minnesota where my father was buried, I read one of the poems she
had written about herself—about what a stubborn and proud woman
she was, and I read something I had written, something about the
fact that she wanted to be remembered for doing the best she could.
The whole ceremony seemed so little. It was raining and cold that
June morning, but it was a time of new moon, the rabbi said, a good
sign, a time for renewal. Maybe he meant for the dead and the living.
They lowered her coffin, flown in from California the night before,
next to my dad's. He had died when I was young and had my whole
life ahead of me. She died when I was approaching old age, with my
wildest adventures and dreams behind me. I couldn't help but think
of their deaths as bookends to my life.

BOOKENDS

They drop my mother's pine coffin
into the space next to my father.
I was so young when they lowered him—no pity
for my mother left to dance alone
or my father who died too soon,
barely pity for myself—fatherless,
what was to come.

So eager to begin my life—
too dumb to imagine
what that meant—lost wedding rings,
babies, wanting in the middle of the night,
crying that went on for years.

But this death, I'm closing in
on the other end.
I understand pity, how much
we have to lose even after

it's all lost. Regret, too,
that my mother and I never found words
to cover the horror in each other's lives,
how carefully we glued the struts of our shadows,
like the balsam models
my brother assembled endlessly.

I was 17 the first time, a virgin
on the eve of living, hair thick—hardly time to say good-bye
to the living or the dead. This time
I have time.

Diane Sher Lutovich

That night I flew back to California. I was immediately struck by the fact that I wouldn't be calling my mother that night or in the morning to tell her I was back, that the trip was good, her friends say hello, the weather was not too bad, and my father's grave looked well taken care of. I was stunned to remember that her phone was disconnected and she was gone. I wondered suddenly if I would ever get used to that absence.

Surprising feelings started surfacing, feelings I thought long since taken care of: sorrow and anger for the seemingly narrow and passive way she had lived her life; little girl feelings—why didn't she, how she didn't. . . . I was about fifteen years old and regressing rapidly. None of these moods lasted long, but they surprised me. I had lived alone most of my life, raised my daughter as a single parent, had a successful business—and I still wanted my mother. Her death not only left a hole in my life, it also forced me to take another look at my relationships with others. Certain things I had done because she wanted me to. I had to reevaluate what I owed to whom. Oh, there were many issues.

I cannot say I was devastated at her death, but there were times out of the blue I'd be suddenly overwhelmed by sorrow, tears, regrets, longing, sadness. It could be something as obvious as seeing an older woman about her size walking hand in hand with her daughter. It might be reflecting on something I bought ("Mom would like this") or something I did ("Mom would approve"). When my daughter threw her arms around me and said, "You're such a generous mom," I was struck with emotion. Why hadn't I done the same with my mother?

One day, a year or two after my mother died, my daughter wanted me to get rid of a piece of furniture that, although ugly, still had some years left. I told her that Grandma (who believed in using everything completely) wouldn't like that. She said, with some mixture of sarcasm and compassion, "But Mom, I have news for you, Grandma's dead." And I said to her, "I have news for you. A mother's voice doesn't stop just because she's dead. You, too, will hear me after I've died. Just like I hear Grandma. Sorry, but you're stuck with me, in one form or another, for the rest of your life."

MOURNING—A PROCESS

When preparing to write this book, I found it difficult to know how to organize the chapters, which topic to deal with first, which second, and third. The difficulty lies in the nature of the mourning process itself, which is neither logical nor linear. Do we feel grief before guilt? Which do we deal with first, our memories of our mother, or our relationships with our siblings? The various aspects of mourning do not follow a specified time frame, especially the feelings and experiences as we work through our grief and accommodate our loss.

To envision the mourning process, instead of a straight line think of concentric circles, each of them very large, with your mother in the center. There are circles dealing with memories, your relationship, grief, guilt, loss, awareness that you are next in line, and so on. Because each of these circles overlaps, you keep moving back and forth, never knowing for sure where one set of feelings will take you. But wherever they take you, they are all a necessary part of the process of mourning.

It might start with hearing a song your mother loved. This memory evokes the picture of your mother sitting alone on a too-long evening listening to the music. That image, in turn, might arouse guilt that you were not able to make her life happier. And that guilt might lead to anger—why didn't she do more to make her own life better? And that might lead to remembering all the reasons she couldn't and the things she was able to do to make your life better. And that might lead you back to loss—she will never again be there to listen to your story or fill in your history.

Each one of these circles deserves attention. By the time you have fully experienced all the emotions, you will be ready for the next stage of your life—taking the best part of her with you and discarding the parts that didn't serve her and don't serve you.

Books, of course, are linear and so the following chapters are laid out in an order that follows more or less a chronological sequence. Yet I would encourage anyone reading this book while experiencing her own process of mourning to read each chapter in whatever order makes the most sense at the time.

REFERENCES

1. M. S. Moss and S. Z. Moss, *The Final Transition,* Baywood, Amityville, New York, 1995.
2. A. Rosberger, *When a Parent Dies,* World Book: Health and Medical Annual, Chicago, Illinois, 1996.
3. S. de Beauvoir, *A Very Easy Death,* Pantheon Books, New York, 1965.

CHAPTER 1

Mothers and Daughters

It's a new trend: Mothers and daughters going into their old age together. Family memberships in AARP. Across the country there are retirement homes in which mothers and daughters live side by side. In many cases, they have not lived so close to each other for fifty years. One enters her seventies, the other moves through her nineties. They've probably never had so much in common.

It is something we're going to see more of. According to *The New York Times Magazine,* March 9, 1997, greater longevity is one of the striking developments of the century—increasing more in the last 100 years than in the prior 5,000, since the Bronze Age. In 1900, life expectancy at birth in America was forty-nine. Today it is seventy-six, and people who have reached fifty-five can expect to live into their eighties. Add to that the fact that twice as many Americans were born in 1955 as in 1935 and it's easy to see that between now and the year 2030, the number of people over sixty-five will almost double. In short, more old people with more aging children.

This means that daughters are involved with their mothers for a larger portion of their lives, with multiple points of interaction and, consequently, more intensely than ever before. Some reasons for the intensity of the mother-daughter relationship have been there all along: the special bond between mother and daughter; the role modeling that mothers perform for their adult daughters; the fact that women are widowed more frequently than men and less apt to remarry; and daughters' proclivity to serve as designated caretakers for their aging mothers. Other reasons for the interaction are new, reflecting changing living patterns, such as divorce and greater personal mobility, which often combine to make parents the most stable reference point in their adult child's life.

MOTHER-DAUGHTER CONNECTION

The relationships mothers have with their daughters are just not the same as the ones they have with their sons. Psychologists studying mother-infant interaction have noted that most mothers treat their male and female infants differently from the moment of birth. It is suggested that women identify more strongly with their daughters, and consequently do not establish the same boundaries. The psychic space between them may be virtually indiscernible.

It is not surprising, then, that psychologist Martha Robbins observed that although the bond between mother and daughter may become weakened, barbed, even torn, it never can be undone [1, p. 246]. That's why so often, even when daughters rebel, their rebellions are often just a "time-out" from their involvement with their mothers. They almost always return with a need to reconnect in some way. If it's true that ego boundaries between mothers and their daughters are less well defined than between mothers and sons, it explains why mothers and daughters so often develop a mutual empathy. From their earliest years, daughters tend to be more sensitive to and aware of the needs of their mothers. And this leads, at least on the part of so many women I talked with, to a need to try to make their mothers happy, to make up for what is missing or wrong in their lives. It is understandable, then, that the daughters feel responsible, too, for their mothers' last years. Sarah believes that, at least unconsciously, she was raised to fill the role of her mother's caretaker. She learned to read her mother's moods, feelings, and reactions probably before she could read her own. Sarah explained that she felt her mother saw her as her special property; her mother had no respect for her boundaries or privacy, and felt she could pry into Sarah's life, even tell her what she was feeling. In explaining a similar situation, Suzanne remembered that this intrusiveness instilled in her, along with resentment, a certain sense of obligation that her brother did not share. As a woman of her time, Suzanne's mother knew that men (even small boys) were special, while women (especially small girls) were not. So while her brother could disappear for hours with no questions asked, Suzanne had to immediately recount everything she had done between the time she left the house and the time she returned. She felt rewarded for being so open and available, while her brother was rewarded for being removed and independent.

This availability is not only a result of these transparent boundaries, it can also be the cause of still greater closeness. Suzanne said that she grew up worrying about her mother's depressions and her father's gambling. She tried to be the good child, to make up for whatever was missing in her mother's life. Her brothers, she said, were either unaware of their parents' problems or felt those problems had nothing to do with them. In the same way, when Vivian mentioned to her brother how worried she used to be about their mother's depression when they were children, he asked, "What depression?"

In my case, I know my mother and brother were close, but when it was time for him to retire and move to a warmer climate, she came to me. She said that she always knew I would be the one she would come to for her last years. Of course, the seeds were planted when I was the little girl playing around her feet, asking her to reassure me that she loved me.

SHARED EXPERIENCE

Shared life experiences serve to reinforce this special connection between mothers and daughters. In fact, daughters often have more contact with their mothers after leaving home than they would have imagined, even when they've moved more than one time zone away, as a majority of the women I talked with had done. Many of these experiences have to do, of course, with such traditionally designated "women's work" as raising children, preparing family meals, preserving family traditions and connections, and keeping the home. Those daughters who had children found their mothers to be a primary source of information on child rearing, which for many remained a central task until middle age.

Madeline recalled that the reconnection with her mother started when she was in labor. She felt not only a connection to all women—past and future—but specifically to her own mother. Sukie had felt estranged from her mother, but felt all the old antagonisms and irritations melt away when her mother arrived after the birth of her first child to tell her stories about her own birth, show her the best ways to change diapers, and bring her the baby to nurse. These stories support Jung's belief that every woman extends backwards into her mother and forward into her daughter.

Mothers share other skills as well: the recipe for *the* angel food cake served at each special occasion, what to do when the curtains are scorched, how to iron a collar, or make preserves. Mothers handed down the family secrets and showed their daughters what it means to be an adult woman. In some cases it doesn't matter what the daughter asks for—her requests for information merely disguising a need for her mother's comfort and support as she attempts to fulfill her many roles. I vividly remember calling to ask my mother about a turkey stuffing recipe the day before I was to have a breast biopsy. I couldn't tell her what was worrying me, because it would upset her and cause me greater distress. I just needed to hear her voice.

And there is the biological connection. Many have noted that no matter how hard we try, the genetic link is just not possible to avoid. Certainly part of this is obvious when looking in the mirror. It is interesting that when we are young, our features seem to have many precedents: "She looks like Aunt Sarah; she has her grandmother's hair; her nose is from her father's side of the family." As we age, however, everything seems to collapse into one gene pool, and middle-aged women are apt to start looking more and more like their mothers.

It goes deeper than looks, of course. Sukie says that she often hears her mother's words coming out of her own mouth. She adds that she has many of the same propensities her mother had at her age—to fear trying something new, to be overly cautious about getting involved with others, to distrust most people, to avoid new responsibilities. She says the only reason she has not become her mother is that she works very hard to cut off those impulses that she feels compromised her mother's life. She makes every effort to learn new things, meet new people, and assume new obligations.

CHANGING LIVING PATTERNS

Ironically, the mobile society in which we live has fostered a certain kind of parent-child intimacy, even intensified it. With families moving so frequently, often the only real place we can call home is the household in which we lived with our parents. After divorce (an event that occurred in the lives of more than 50 percent of the women I interviewed), parents remained one of the few constants on which a daughter could rely. Ultimately, since women usually outlive men, it is the mother who is the last connection to the childhood home. The marital bond, though more intense for most adults, has proved in recent decades to be quite fragile. It is not unusual for recently divorced persons to seek and receive considerable parental support—emotional as well as financial. In fact, three of the women I interviewed returned to live with their parents after their divorce until they could regroup. Few would suggest that the severance of parental bonds has or will approach the soaring divorce rate. But while husbands and children come and go, Mom stays.

Even when the daughter and mother do not live close to one another, there are more ways to stay in contact than ever before. The advent of e-mail and fast, relatively cheap phone calls makes distance all but irrelevant. Whereas my mother, influenced by the Depression, limited herself to one three-minute long-distance call a week, I am apt to talk to my daughter every day, no matter what time zone she is living in.

DAUGHTER AS MOTHER'S CARETAKER

A lifetime of involvement prepares us for the final scenario—the one in which a daughter cares for her aging mother. In fact, E. Shanas, as reported by Kowalski, found that, next to the spouse, an adult daughter is the most likely person to be the primary care giver for an older person at home. A recent study of families in the Cleveland, Ohio, area who were providing home care for elderly members found that the spouse was the primary care giver in 50 percent of the cases, a daughter in 41 percent, a son in 4.5 percent, and a daughter-in-law in 4 percent [2, p. 189]. This is, of course, also in keeping with the belief that it is the woman's role to nurture the family and care for elderly parents when they are sick. (Other studies show that not only is it the daughter who is singled out as the primary caregiver, it is usually either the oldest or youngest daughter.)

Widowhood, which means the loss of companionship and care a spouse usually provides, is the lot of more women than men because of longer female life expectancy and the tendency for the wife to be the younger partner in marriage. In fact, women over sixty-five are three times as likely as men to be widowed. According to Census Bureau estimates for 1999, women over sixty-five outnumber men by almost 30 percent: 20,250,000 women to 14,189,000 men. Women over eighty-five years old outnumber men by about 38 percent: 2,945,000 women to 1,179,000 men. Moreover, women are more likely than men to be restricted in their capacity to take care of themselves.

A generation ago it was unusual for a sixty-year-old woman to have a mother still alive, but it is and will continue to be a more common phenomenon if current projections are accurate. My mother was fifty-three when her mother died at eighty-five. I was fifty-seven when my mother died at ninety-one. Many have commented on the fact that our country is growing older by the decade and that many of our parents have outlived their own parents by ten or twenty years. I can count among my close acquaintances at least ten women over sixty whose widowed mothers are not only still alive, but thriving well into their late eighties and nineties. If one peruses the obituary page, it is striking to read the ages of the deceased, particularly the women—many close to 100. They leave behind daughters, often in their seventies, to say nothing of granddaughters and great grand-daughters. The oldest women I interviewed was seventy-seven. Her mother had recently died at ninety-eight.

Women are more apt to be alone in their later years, not only because of their increased longevity and younger age at marriage, but also because they remarry far less often than men. Widowers over sixty-five are seven times as likely to remarry as widows. So it is not surprising that the mothers of approximately 80 percent of the women I talked with outlived their husbands by many years, some by as many as forty years. Of the few mothers who had remarried, most had done so while their daughters were still living at home. In the majority of those cases, the second husband had also predeceased the mother.

There might be still another reason why so many older women are alone. This entrenched widowhood could be a sign of the times in which these women lived. One woman said when she asked her mother why she had chosen to live alone for so many years, never making any effort to meet another man, her mother told her that after her husband died, she vowed never again to be in the position of letting someone tell her what to do. Perhaps others felt this, too, and so these women, given the choice, preferred to be alone. (Patriarchy might be dying, but it has left a lot of single women in its wake.)

With all of the mother-daughter connections, then, and the incidence of women living longer and alone, it is not surprising that after a lifetime of daughter turning to mother, mothers often turn to their daughters to provide a wide range of material, social, and emotional support, even if it means moving. Although many of the women I spoke with said their mothers had remained in the family home or at least in the same community after their husbands died, as their support system diminished over time, they felt it necessary to be near at least one of their children, usually their daughters.

Accordingly, the interviews revealed that in almost all cases, whether or not by choice, the daughters were more involved than their brothers with their mothers' final days. Vivian reported with some irritation that, even though she had job responsibilities and as many obligations as her brother, she was the one her mother called when she had a medical appointment or when she needed something. For a long time she hesitated to ask her mother why that was the case. When she finally did, her mother explained that as much as she loved her son, she didn't feel she had the right to bother him. Nor did she have the same assurance he would drop what he was doing to care for her. She knew she could depend on her daughter. A double-edge, the son's work more important, the daughter more accessible and dependable.

Of course there were exceptions. Bea had always made it clear, at least from the time of her marriage, she wanted as much distance as possible from her mother. In her case, her two brothers were the caretakers for their mother. Yet it is worth noting that of the nineteen women in this study who had brothers, only five mentioned their brothers playing a significant part in their mothers' final care. Since fewer than 50 percent of the women I interviewed had brothers, however, this observation has only limited relevance in terms of this study.

It is certainly possible that, as women start expecting the same emotional responsiveness of their sons as they do of their daughters, and as men become more involved in parenting, men will become more equally involved in caring for aging parents. The numbers, however, are not yet in on that one.

SHIFTING MEANINGS OF DEATH

In some ways, society's isolation of death and the dying contributes to the trauma of the event. Even in the early part of this century, death was an integral part of life, not pushed off to the corner. People used to die at home (thanks to hospice, this is again becoming more common) and were also laid out there. The proximity of the dead may have required an extensive grieving process on the part of family and friends in order to differentiate clearly the living from the dead, but everyone understood its importance. In contemporary society, on the other hand, the worlds of the living and the dead have been artificially separated and the grieving process has diminished in importance. Consequently, those who grieve are apt to find less support than mourners a generation ago.

We have too few reminders today of death's solemnity. Many of us return to work directly from the funeral or after the three days usually allowed for bereavement leave. It's "life as usual." How can we truly mourn the loss of life and rejoice in the gift of life when we don't take the time to feel it? We tend to downplay grief's significance or "stuff it down" where it gets heavier and heavier.

Another aspect of this rush to get things back to normal is that the death of anyone, especially our mother, reminds us that the bell will someday toll for us. Unable to imagine a time when they will not be alive, when everything will stop for them, people often welcome an opportunity to hide from the reality of death. So avoidance becomes the only way to deal with it. In this way, the pain of loss is mitigated, limited in the short-term, but so is the possibility of growth and transformation that can come with looking at death and all its implications for the living.

SUMMING UP

It is not surprising that daughters find themselves enmeshed in the lives of their elderly mothers. It is the last stage of a process that started with the special bonding between mothers and daughters, continued on through their shared experiences, and concluded with the mother most apt to be elderly and alone. If her mother was to live deep into old age, her daughter might well have been marked as caretaker from the very beginning. And because it is the daughter who is most involved with the final caretaking, it is also to be expected that she is the one who feels most deeply her mother's death.

As society affords us less opportunity to work through our grief and loss, it is up to us to learn what we need for ourselves. By examining the meanings of life's ending—personal, genetic, historical, and societal—we daughters can hope to find the appropriate responses to grieve authentically, meaningfully—as daughters, as friends, even as a society.

REFERENCES

1. M. A. Robbins, *Midlife Women and Death of Mother: A Study of Psychohistorical and Spiritual Transformation,* Peter Lang, New York, 1990.
2. N. Claire Kowalski, Anticipating the Death of an Elderly Parent, in *Loss and Anticipatory Grief,* Therese A. Rando (ed.), Lexington Books, Lexington, Massachusetts, 1986.

CHAPTER 2

Relationships

I had grown very fond of this dying woman. As we talked in the half-darkness I assuaged an old unhappiness; I was renewing the dialogue that had been broken off during my adolescence and that our differences and our likenesses had never allowed us to take up again. And the early tenderness that I had thought dead forever came to life again [1, p. 76].

Some time ago, I called a friend of mine to offer condolences on the death of her mother. She told me, "I'm so glad to be free of her nagging and complaining. She never approved of anything I did and I'm glad it's over."

When I called to offer another woman condolences, she replied tearfully, "I can't believe she's gone. I will never stop wanting to talk to her, to be with her, to touch her. I want my mommy."

Among the daughters I interviewed, the stories of their relationships with their mothers and their feelings upon their deaths were often as divergent as these two responses. In each case, the daughter's perception of herself and her mother depended on so many variables—the period of her life she reflected on, how accepting and nurturing her mother was, the degree to which her mother respected and supported her independence, and how dependent she was on her mother's approval.

It is a given that every woman has a unique history with her mother, especially when that history spans five decades or more. After hearing so many women's stories, it is hard to disagree with Moss when he observes that parent-child bonds are filled with conflict, and that the quality of the relationship depends on how these tensions are woven together [2, p. 105]. The persistence, absence, or resolution of a mother's expectations and needs and those of her daughter especially seem to influence their relationship, at least as reported by the daughter.

During my interviews, there were daughters who did not seem to recall (or at least did not mention) conflicts between themselves and their mothers, while others vividly remembered (sometimes to the exclusion of any other memories) an unhappy and irreconcilable relationship. Often those tensions that had to do with the daughters' need to break away from their mothers in order to become their own persons were eventually resolved or at least transformed by the daughter's mature understanding of her mother. Those tensions, however, that arose from deeply held, life-long dissatisfactions and disappointments frequently were not.

THE STORIES

When asked about their relationship with their mothers, daughters tended to focus on significant memories and impressions, often just fragments, the way a life is remembered over time. "She used to tell me over and over how glad she was I was her daughter." "I'll never forget the time she stopped talking to me for three weeks because I lost my watch." "She always seemed to be disappointed in me." "She wanted me to live with her forever."

Some daughters recalled their earliest memories, some their last. Some stories highlighted their struggle to escape their mothers' influence; others stressed the importance of their reconciliation. For the most part, the relationships were not static but reflected changes associated with the daughter's growing maturity and need for independence, her self-discovery, her ability to understand her mother in a new way, or to accept her for who she was.

Daughters' memories of the mother-daughter relationships can be divided into four chapters: childhood, adolescence, adulthood, and the mother's decline and death. For some of these daughters, each "chapter" is different: a loving childhood, a conflict-ridden adolescence, a reconciliation during adulthood, and love and caring at the time of the mother's death. In this last chapter, some women who had been estranged from their mothers were fortunate enough to rediscover their early affection, as Simone de Beauvoir did. Others had always held their mothers in high esteem and affection, and were able to express this at the end. Others, bitter after decades of alienation, buried their mothers with relief and without regret.

Several daughters characterized their relationship as free from conflict. They not only have fond memories of their childhood, but appeared to have survived the adolescent rebellion stage without clearly defined periods of tension or separation. This category includes daughters who enjoyed close, loving relationships all their lives as well as daughters who were not particularly close to their mothers. In both cases, the demands and expectations of mother and daughter appear to have been well matched and mutually satisfying.

Ella, the oldest of three daughters, recalled her relationship with her mother as consistently loving. She always felt very close to her mother, even though she lived at some distance much of her adult life. Two main themes came through when she spoke of her relationship with her mother: how supportive her mother was and how much her mother loved children. The strongest thread throughout Ella's story was of the great respect and love she had for her mother. "My mother was always there for me. Even when I went through my rebellious period, she handled it very well." She stated that one of the reasons their relationship was so positive was that they were always careful with one another. "My mother was always a moderating force," Ella recalls, "and even though there was the normal adolescent friction, there was no major alienation."

For a while, Ella lived in Europe where her own daughter was born. When she returned to the States and divorced, "I couldn't have asked for more supportive parents." For a time, she lived with her parents and she remembered, "My mother and daughter had a phenomenal relationship. My mother was really into kids and at the same time she was very much into women's and children's issues." Even when Ella received welfare, which upset her father, her mother was right there saying "It's the duty of the state—we have nothing to be sorry about."

When Ella's mother, at seventy-seven, was diagnosed with a very aggressive form of cancer, she tried to remain independent for as long as possible. Once the cancer metastasized, she refused the option of more chemotherapy. Faced with only two months to live, Ella said, her mother went to live with Ella's sister, and Ella and her other sister joined them. "As horrible as it was, we all got to know her—she was open and honest with her feelings. All of us had renewed respect for her—we didn't know she could be that strong."

Dorie adored her mother and said that she and her mother were always extremely close—while she was young, when she was growing up, as an adult, and when her mother was dying. "My mother was very private, but I think we really understood each other. I thought she was a saint, a flawed, human saint—one who was completely and unconditionally loving. Nothing was ever a problem; she loved me. She loved everyone—no judgment—just her nature, so sweet-natured." Dorie believed her own experience with cancer ten years earlier enabled her to identify with what her mother was going through and that the shared experience made it easier for her mother to trust her.

Dorie said that she felt lucky to be with her mother as she was dying and felt "blessed, in fact, to have two months staring at my mother, so beautiful to me, to be able to touch her, rub her hair, her body." If she hadn't been able to spend that time with her mother, Dorie said, "it would have been terrible for me and for her." She said that she did everything she could for her mother and that though, "I was not perfect, I was okay."

Gena was one of the daughters whose relationships with their mothers was tempered by the fact that they lived apart from each other. In Gena's case it was due to her husband's work. She reported no major rift or separation with her mother, and was very aware of what they had in common and their differences. She chose to focus on their similarities. "We had some really good conversations. My mother and I were the most alike in the family in terms of our interests. We both taught English (Mom was a teacher's assistant although she never finished college) and she was very well read. I remember some of the book conversations—she loved Southern writers. I tried to get her to read others. She always encouraged me to be a writer and I encouraged her to be a writer."

Gena said that her mother was not a practical person and that her father had to manage everything. She described her mother as a "Southern belle" and a talented pianist who grew up believing practicing was her job. "She just practiced. She was not an easy person and a very temperamental one." Gena saw herself as the independent one among the three daughters. "I aligned myself with my father and felt much closer to him." During summers, she would go with her father to visit his parents while her sisters went with their mother to visit her parents.

Gena was sixteen when her youngest sister was born and felt there was a major shift at that point. "My mother had no room in her life for anyone else." Gena said her mother was not well at the time, and, after the birth, spent six months in the hospital.

But still, the relationship seemed good. "As I got older," Gena said, "mother couldn't have had too many daughters, even though from the time I was twenty-three I never lived close by. It was a telephone relationship." She said it was hard because her mother wasn't comfortable having people stay with her.

Four years before her mother died, her parents moved to a community near Gena's home. By that time, she said, her mother "was slipping." For the last two years of her life, she needed constant care. Her doctor diagnosed it as dementia; she had no short-term memory and her bodily functions started failing. There was just one episode after another in which they were forced to see what was happening. "The day before she died, she reached out to Dad and me—she hadn't done that. She gave me a hug. My sister came and she hugged her, and then let go."

Like Gena, Linda's relationship with her mother seems to have been almost conflict free. With the exception of her parents' opposition to her early marriage, Linda and her mother seemed to have had a warm and loving relationship, one that met the needs of both. Linda, the oldest of three daughters, said her mother often told her "how proud I am of my girls." Linda remembered her mother telling her that when she herself was little, her own mother had not loved her and "so she often told us that she would always love us and that we were the most important things in her life and she treated us that way."

Linda remembers her family as the "typical 50's family." Her mother stayed home, made their clothes, and kept house. "None of us were pushed by either of our parents but we were told that the only thing that counts is education. You have to get educated. You have to have something to fall back on in your life."

Linda's only major regret is how unhappy her parents were when she married "too young and to the wrong person. They were always unhappy about that." The man Linda married was Catholic and his family insisted the wedding take place in the Catholic church. "My mother fought that; my parents were totally moral and totally atheistic." Afterward, when Linda moved from New York to California and decided to go to medical school, she knew "they would be thrilled." Throughout her adult life, Linda and her parents remained on opposite coasts, but they saw each other and talked often. Despite the conflict about her marriage, Linda and her parents enjoyed a loving relationship, without anger or tension.

Her mother was seventy-nine and had been in good health when Linda received a message from one of her sisters: "I thought you should know Mama hasn't been feeling well." A second message came from the emergency room saying her mother was not well and there might be some neurological problem. The third message said she was in a coma and it was determined that she had a cerebral aneurism.

At that point Linda flew East. When she arrived, her mother was still in a coma. Her sisters were taking turns with her, talking to her and debating whether she could hear them. Doctors were talking about surgery and no one knew what to do. "So I asked for a comment on percentages and the doctor said there is about 90 percent morbidity . . . I was so glad I had asked the question because all of a sudden everything changed as far as expectations, at least for me." Even with the surgery, the outcome was unclear. It was possible Linda's mother would be wheelchair-bound the rest of her life; she might lose the use of one side of her body. "That's where I knew she would have a problem and I decided I would go back and talk to the neurosurgeon and try to get as accurate a description as I could. I had reservations and plans to fly back and then all of a sudden I got a phone call saying something had happened during the night and essentially she wasn't alive any more; she was literally dead. I can't say I was terribly surprised—I was really dreading the kind of decisions [that had to be made], how she would face her life."

The following morning the family went to obtain approval to turn off the machine. They told Linda what they were doing and that her mother would be dead by the time she got there. Linda accepted that. "When I had left, I felt I would probably never see her again, so I talked to her and said good-bye. I felt good because I did it at a time that she had some consciousness and now she clearly had none. . . . The saddest thing for me was that I didn't have a chance to tell her everything I would have wanted to."

Koru, the fourth of six children born to parents who had emigrated from Japan, also had a comfortable if somewhat restrained relationship with her mother. About ten years before her death, Koru's mother developed Parkinson's disease, and because she was becoming more fragile, Koru's brother and his wife invited their mother to live in the apartment behind their house. A few years after the move, Koru returned from five years abroad; having spent time in India and throughout Asia, she was acutely aware of the importance of family network and support systems. So when Koru found that her mother needed help, without making a conscious decision—"in fact, no decision"—she moved in with her mother so that she could do the cooking. This arrangement lasted for five years until her mother's death. She felt that the arrangement "worked because we were not so close. It was not too intense—she couldn't press my buttons as she did my older sisters'."

Koru explained that there was also a great cultural difference. Her mother basically spoke no English and Koru spoke almost no Japanese. "We didn't communicate heart to heart—at least not verbally." But, she said with pleasure and astonishment, "I learned to anticipate. I was surprised at how much communication there was without any verbal exchange." She wished her mother had said more but took comfort in the fact that, "I knew her at that place in time." Being with her "gave me a sense of balance, security, place, comfort—it was not all one way. I can't understand when people said to me after she died, 'Now you can get on with your own life.' That *was* my life. I didn't put anything on hold—you don't do that thinking you have your life on hold." Koru was there when her mother died at home.

BREAKING FREE

Among those daughters who did encounter conflict with their mothers, some were fortunate enough to find within themselves or their relationships the means to successfully resolve these issues. Most often, the essential conflict arose from the daughters' need for independence from their parents' influence in order to come into their own as adults.

Cory left home at the age of eighteen because she and her mother were "two strong Irish women who couldn't budge." Her mother told her she would have to see less of the young man she had been dating. Cory remembered telling her, "In that case, I just won't come home," and her mother replied, "That's up to you."

Cory, nine years younger than her closest sibling, said she always felt wonderfully anticipated. Because her parents were so much older when she was born, she said it was almost like belonging to another generation. She said she was very surprised by her own decision to move since "My mother and I had never locked horns. The rules were strict in my house and I always followed them." Cory had never been rebellious or defiant, and was always happy to be at home, so much so, in fact, that her oldest brother took her aside and told her she should leave. Otherwise, he warned, she might end up staying with her parents until she was forty, since they didn't want her to leave and she showed no signs of wanting greater independence.

Once she moved out, her mother wrote to her every day. Whenever Cory went to visit, her mother would introduce her as "the baby we wish would come back here." Each time, Cory said, she "winced with the guilt of it all."

Her mother's stroke was a surprise. Cory received a call early on a Friday morning from one of her sisters saying she had found their mother on the living room floor. Cory immediately made arrangements to fly home. Since her mother was conscious and appeared stable, she decided to fly back Saturday morning. By the time she arrived, her mother was no longer conscious. Cory and her siblings spent the day discussing what measures they might take to prolong her life; Cory was surprised at how much in agreement they were about what they should do. They decided they would go out to eat together, since the doctor told them their mother was in a plateau and could be there for some time. As soon as they finished their meal, they received a call from the nurse telling them their mother had died. Afterwards, Cory said, assisting in the plans for her mother's funeral helped to make up for the fact she had not been with her mother when she was first stricken or when she died.

Marcia's strongest memories are of how much she loved her mother when she was a little girl and how "paralyzed" she became whenever her mother left the house. "I remember being aghast at being sent away from home, which was quite often—to camp and then to boarding school when I was fourteen. I was really in love with her." Marcia's parents were Canadian with English roots and "I was brought up in that English style where your parents weren't around much and you were raised by others. I felt my mother really wanted to be a mother, that that was more important to her and she really fought to be with us." When she was with her mother, Marcia "felt loved, protected, that I was important. I was her little darling."

Marcia thought her mother was forever disappointed that she didn't stay close to home. Once Marcia left for boarding school, she never returned home to live. Her mother would tell her that she was never sending anyone else away to school.

Aside from her memories of being an adored child and how much her mother missed her, Marcia remembered the power struggles they got into. "I often felt she didn't like me, essentially who I was. She would have liked me to be a softer person, and I wanted to be that, too, but I just couldn't." Marcia reported she had a "hard time" with her mother when she was in her twenties. "I was pretty cruel to her and sided with my father in his new marriage. I needed to do some breaking away." But in her thirties, when Marcia divorced, her mother was very supportive, taking the children and helping in many ways.

Marcia felt that through the years she often disappointed her mother, "but I think it was because she couldn't stand up to my own power, my need to tell everyone what to do and how to do it. Her way of dealing with me was to step in my way."

When her mother was diagnosed with liver cancer, Marcia was there, taking care of her, arranging for help, making sure everything ran smoothly. Because her mother never acknowledged she was dying, Marcia didn't talk about it with her. One of the things Marcia regretted is that she never had a chance to say good-bye. Before her next visit, she received a call that her mother had died the night before.

Although Marcia did not have the chance to plan the funeral, which was all done according to the church, she did break with tradition in reading a piece she had written about her mother. It was a chance for her to talk about her mother's kindness and generosity, how much she was loved, and how much she would be missed. Marcia also was able to point to her own granddaughter, who was blond like her great grandmother and shared her disposition. Proof, Marcia pointed out, "that it all keeps going."

Jordana is one of those daughters who truly had to turn her back on her mother before she could be at peace with herself and their relationship. Growing up, Jordana said, her mother's attachment to her was so great, it felt like the "invasion of the body snatchers." Jordana's rebellion took the form of vomiting after breakfast for years. "My mother was so unfulfilled herself, so self-effacing that she had to live vicariously through me. . . . She was a shadow, a two-dimensional person, I was just here as someone to protect and to give her what pleasure I could." Jordana said she knows her mother admired her, loved her in an "adoring way but she had little to give me, at least little of what a child needs." Jordana said, "I just became the family's pet."

Jordana freed herself of her mother's grip after she divorced her first husband and took part in a psychodrama workshop. "I was able to cut the cord, to get rid of her symbolically. And that enabled me to become myself." She said that it was a long struggle to exorcise the early mother, but "I have felt completely separate for the last twenty-five years. Once I was reborn as myself, I could not be angry and could form some kind of truce. I was able to acknowledge that she did the best she could and gave me a lot, not some of the things children need, though. She wanted my confidence which she never got—never intimacy—just a kind of truce of appreciation of what we could give each other."

Jordana lived near her mother and saw her often. Her death was wholly unexpected; there was no advance warning that anything was wrong. Her mother choked on a sandwich while out to lunch. She was taken to the hospital where it was determined that she had a "stricture" at the base of her esophagus. One thing led to another and within a week she had died from pneumonia. During that time, Jordana's mother made it clear she was too miserable to live and Jordana reported this to the rest of the family.

Jordana remembered that the family was in agony watching the various procedures doctors tried, and finally Jordana, her father, and brother agreed there was no point in prolonging her life. Jordana said, "My children, the people she loved most and who loved her most, finally all agreed she wasn't going to lick it." She said it was a horrible choice to make: "I didn't want to be grownup and be responsible. I wouldn't have done it differently but it was terrible." Jordana perceived the whole process of making the decision as a role reversal—the child making that life or death decision for her parent.

Annie is another woman who felt her mother did not answer her needs because of her own early life experiences. She explained, "Until I was a teenager, I never questioned anything she said. And then I went through a rebellious stage." Much of that had to do "with my recognition of how little I got from her in terms of support or understanding of my life. I mostly felt distant for a big part of life and yet I was the one she encouraged to go beyond the narrow world in which we lived. She had wanted more for herself and singled me out to achieve what she didn't, but I also felt resentment and that had to do with her anger and bitterness."

Later, once she understood more about the reasons behind her mother's anger, Annie found it easier to reconcile. She said her mother was a "traumatized, emotionally impaired, damaged person." Annie saw that as a result of her mother's early life in Europe where she was orphaned and separated from her siblings, she always felt a profound sense of alienation. She said, "I have recollections of going to her with a problem and my mother would reply, 'You think you have problems, I'll tell you what is on my heart.'" Annie early on learned not to go to her with any problems.

Annie explained that ten years before her mother died, with the help of very good therapy, "I began to understand the relationship with my mother and make peace. I gained a profound recognition of the impact of my mother on my life in spite of my years of alienation. I did come to recognize how different my life would have been if she had not had a sense of the possibilities and identified me as the person to realize them. It was a burden as well as a gift. Ultimately I had an overpowering sense of gratitude. I know she made it possible for me to become the person I am. She made it okay for me to want more."

Annie was with her when her mother was dying. Because of Annie's success in the "real world" it was up to her to make the final decisions about "heroic measures" and, once her mother died, to plan the funeral. This was a position she was marked for fifteen years earlier when her mother turned over the finances to her. "I was the only one who had a college education. I was seen as the smart one in the family and my mother depended on me even though she, herself, was an amazingly smart business woman."

Her mother had signed a living will but the hospital didn't accept it, and so when the time came, Annie had to make some "agonizing decisions" about her mother's care. "My older sister at first wanted to prolong life in whatever way possible. My feeling was that there could be no recovery. There was very little responsiveness, so it came down to the issue of a feeding tube. The doctor said with a tube we could keep her alive for three years."

Her younger sister was conflicted but sided more with her older sister. Annie then spoke to a rabbi who pointed out that once you intervene, you cannot reverse the decision: once you put in a tube, you cannot later remove it. Annie said, "I then decided to do nothing and moved her back to the nursing home where she died the same day."

Conflicts in mother-daughter relationships are more the norm than exception. Many of the daughters, like Jordana and Annie, had been able to leave earlier conflicts behind, but that was not true for all daughters. In fact, in describing the development of parent-child relationships over time, Moss states, "old conflicts indigenous to the relationship may persist with issues of control and blaming often recurring. New conflicts are then superimposed upon the old" [2, p. 106].

Some, of course, did continue with issues of blaming and control. Most, however, did not. This, I suspect, has something to do with the fact that so many of the daughters were trying new ways of being with their elderly mothers, the availability of outside help, and/or just because everyone had grown so old. Certainly, in my case, I had already proven my independence and I had worked through any need to blame. My mother, too, long ago gave up her need for control. And though she might have still blamed me for moving so far away, by the end she was just grateful to have a daughter who would look after and care for her. Twenty years earlier, the picture might have been different.

Sarah, however, was one who did find that conflicts with her mother in adulthood compounded the earlier tensions. "I was very close to my mother and she to me when I was growing up. She was a wonderful, creative person with great ideas." But Sarah also remembers her mother as being "a bit smothering." Sarah explained that her mother didn't have much of a sense of boundary and impinged on her daughter's privacy. Adding to the intensity was the fact that "I was her main emotional support." She thinks that a key event in their relationship occurred when she was about eleven and her mother went through a period of crisis for two or three years. Her father had fallen in love with someone else and talked about leaving. "He didn't talk about it to me, but she did. She was very needy during that time and used me as a confidante. We had always enjoyed great rapport but during that time it was very painful and wrenching. The good news was that I felt very needed. On the other hand, I felt her need was so great and I didn't know how to reject her. That knowledge—and resentment for her intrusiveness—came much later. I just felt it was my responsibility to be available for her."

Sarah said that when she was younger, "to keep that gentle voice, that feeling of being loved, was very precious to me—my mother could be so much fun and so generous and so warm that I just learned to accept all of her love. I just learned to be her good girl. I felt I was her favored child and I had no idea what I gave up in the process."

Once Sarah recognized that by being her mother's "good girl," she had given up her own voice, her integrity, and the need to be herself, the relationship changed. Shortly before her mother started her final decline, Sarah returned to the East Coast to live with her mother until she found her own home. During that time, Sarah did everything in her power to care for her. At some point, Sarah surmised, her mother must have become very angry. Without telling Sarah, she changed her will so the house went to both Sarah and her brother, even though she had always told Sarah the house would be hers. Sarah didn't discover this change until after her mother had died. She said that she felt hurt, anger, and sadness, and it was only then that she recognized how angry her mother had been. "We were living together and I was being ornery and obdurate and not being her good girl." She thinks her mother changed her will once Sarah was "no longer flowing like water around my mother's feelings."

Sarah said that in planning the memorial service—something she considered to be a great experience—her anger at her mother gradually gave way to disappointment. And finally, the disappointment mixed with all the happy memories of an earlier time. Sarah was able to make her peace with her mother's memory.

Carla, an only child, always got a mixed message from her mother—that she was at once a most wanted child and that she was a "hateful child." On the one hand, she felt very special and lucky, and on the other, that she had been born into the wrong family. Carla said her mother "was a loving and giving person. I have the feeling of having been a huge disappointment and I always wondered how I got in this family." She thinks her mother felt this, too; she used to say to her, "You're not at all like me." Not surprisingly, ambivalence characterized every aspect of their relationship.

Carla said that she did not feel close to either parent. "They were such staunch Republicans and Southern Baptists, so much stricter than other parents." She felt resentful that there were so many things she was not allowed to do and because they had such a "black and white way of looking at the world." Even so, Carla said, "Mother was wonderful." She did good things, like volunteering in the hospital, and was a "good, kind, generous person." Carla remembered her mother's ultimatums and the conflicts, like the time she forbade her daughter to move to New York and then gave her the money to do so. Another part of the estrangement was precipitated by Carla's divorce. Her mother was ashamed and didn't want anyone to know.

Carla said she always tried to be a good daughter. She remembered writing her mother letters telling her how wonderful she was and getting no response. Ultimately, it came down to the fact that "I didn't live the life my parents wanted for me and so I was living a lie as far as my mother was concerned." It seemed mutual. Carla said, "She always thought the worst of me." The other side is that "I never told her anything. I took a perverse pleasure in not sharing my life. I just rejected their life."

Things changed after her mother's first stroke. According to Carla, her mother was nice and so happy her daughter was there. (Several daughters commented on how much sweeter their mothers became after a stroke.) Then about a year later, another stroke followed. At that point, when she went back to see her, her mother could no longer talk and had started dying. Carla didn't know if her mother even knew who she was, and she was almost sorry she came. Her mother stopped eating, and the doctors told Carla her mother was starving to death. Doctors put in a feeding tube, but her brain stopped functioning. At that time, they decided not to put her on a respirator. Carla said that through the whole thing, it was so hard to make decisions; she had no support, no way of knowing if she was doing the right thing. What Carla found interesting about that second stroke was that her mother, who had never liked to touch or be touched, wanted to hold her daughter's hand. She was glad of that because, "I never had that contact with my mother."

Carla was not there when her mother died, although she had wanted to be. Her mother died suddenly, a week before Carla's next visit.

TENSIONS UNRESOLVED

Lana's conflicts with her mother were never resolved. She had been angry at her mother since she was a young girl and nothing changed with her mother's death. "She died three days before my daughter got married. I was furious with her; she did it on purpose," she says somewhat facetiously. She adds, "I had a good time at the wedding."

Lana explains that she left home at eighteen. "I was always more angry than anything else. She was never motherly, never warm, loving or caring. I think she was very jealous. She had been the only woman before I came along, and then did her best to keep me down. I guess she taught me what I wanted to know but she was never the mother I wanted."

Lana said her mother always hated the small Iowa town in which they lived and she suffered from frequent migraines. "They seemed to be my fault for being sassy or something like that—or maybe I didn't behave properly. So it was my job to bring the wash cloths, to apologize, to promise to never do it again, though I knew I would. She used to always say to me when I resented something she did or didn't do, 'Well you don't know what happened to me.'" Lana doesn't know if that was to put her off guard or something had actually happened. It was never talked about. She adds "I don't recall her fondly."

No one was with her mother when she died. The nursing home director called Lana's brother who told the director to cremate her and mail him her ashes. About a week later, Lana went to her brother's home and they buried her mother's ashes in his backyard.

Nancy lived in the same California city as her mother, but was not with her when she died due to the suddenness of it. Her relations with her mother were always strained, and Nancy explained that, although she was not angry at her mother, she never found her to be a source of comfort. For one thing, Nancy could never understand why her mother so preferred her sister. As long as she could remember, her mother had favored her older daughter over Nancy.

Another factor in their relationship had to do with the death of Nancy's twenty-two-year-old son, who contracted an infection while trekking around the world. In times of tragedy, a mother's support can strengthen the relationship. Nancy, however, felt her mother was not able to help. This failure added another layer to the disappointment and tension that already existed between them. Nancy was still grieving her son's loss when her mother died five years later. As a result, she felt her mother's death was worthy of little attention and said she couldn't understand why "anyone considered it a big deal."

Unfortunately, there were many daughters who had tension-filled relationships with their mothers that were never resolved during the mothers' lifetime. Yet in most cases, this did not deter them from doing what they could for them. Though the specifics might differ, the pattern is there—daughters disappointed at never having the relationship with their mothers that they wanted yet ready to spend their time and resources to help their mothers make as painless and peaceful an exit as possible. At the end, you couldn't tell these women from those who had nothing but praise and the deepest of affection for their mothers all of their lives.

Sandra is one of these women, disappointed yet caring. She thought her mother was controlling, unsympathetic toward women, and insensitive; against her daughter's express wishes, she kept up a relationship with Sandra's ex-husband. And yet, when her mother was dying, Sandra closed her business to move across country and assist her mother as long as she could.

Barbara thought her mother was "magic," even though she suffered all of her life because her mother was always critical, judgmental, and never found her "good enough." But in Barbara's case, it was her mother who broke with her. After college, Barbara went to Greece with a man from work. She said that her mother "flipped out and tried to stop it. She basically wouldn't speak to me for a year and a half because I had left and because I had gone off with a man. Even when I called her on my birthday, she wouldn't talk to me." Barbara found this silence "very traumatic and I had a breakdown." Once her mother resumed speaking to her, Barbara frequently went back to Florida to visit her mother. When her mother was sick, she tried to help her, but there was nothing she could do for her. Several years after her mother's death, she grieves deeply for her mother and for the relationship they never had.

Barbara's situation, like others', seems to demonstrate the fact that there is often no clear connection between the nature and quality of the mother-daughter relationship and the way they deal with their dying or the grief they experience after their deaths. Memories of a perfect relationship can leave a daughter overwhelmed with grief for the loss of this connection, or grateful she had her mother as long as she did. In the same way, memories of a disappointing relationship can also leave a daughter overwhelmed with grief for the relationship she never had, or grateful "to be free."

A friend used to laugh, death seeming so far away, that she was sure when it was her time to die, her daughter would put her on an ice floe and push her off to sea. Not because she thought her children saw her as an uncaring mother nor excessively critical or smothering. She was just acknowledging how hard it is to know what makes the difference between those daughters who would do anything for their mothers, no matter how unsympathetic the mother might be, and those who would do nothing, no matter how caring and nurturing that mother might be. Maybe it all comes down to intention, to wanting, to knowing that caring for the person who brought you into this world, no matter how flawed your relationship might have been, somehow makes you a more complete person.

SUMMING UP

Given the extent to which each woman—mothers as well as daughters—is unique in her needs, values, and life experiences, it is no wonder that mother-daughter relationships vary so greatly. Nevertheless, in my interviews, certain themes came up over and over that seem to have a profound effect on the quality of the relationship. These have to do with expectations. The more intense the expectations of the mother, the more conflicted the relationship. Those mothers who put great demands on their daughters, whether for love, closeness, or perfection, often drove them away, some temporarily, others permanently. In the same way, mothers whose relationships with their daughters were based on their own unhappiness made close, loving relationships difficult, if not impossible.

Many of those women who went through difficult years with their mothers were lucky enough to have their mothers live long enough so they could "reweave the tensions," an opportunity unavailable to daughters whose mothers die while they are still trying to form their own lives. Some of these daughters found therapy helped them with the insights necessary to form a new relationship with their mothers; some of the daughters moved away, and across miles and years were able to see their mothers in a new way. Others learned about new kinds of relationships by watching their own adult children struggle to make their own lives. For still others, it was just the blessing of years, of maturing. However they came to it, they found a way to reconcile with their mothers at some deep level. They had a chance to close the circle before it was too late. But even those daughters who had not reconnected in the deepest sense also wanted to be with their mothers during their final weeks or months. Something in them, maybe loyalty, maybe thinking "this could be me," urged them to drop everything so that they could be available to their mothers. They may not have felt as complete as those who had reconnected early, but they took satisfaction in what they did, and acknowledged they could not have forgiven themselves if they had not done what they could. And, of course, those daughters who had always felt love for their mothers felt gratified to be able to give this final, important aid to their mothers.

Those who managed, either because of or in spite of their relationship, to be there for their mothers reported feeling fortunate to have had the chance. Only those women who had failed to reconcile and to forgive, were seemingly unavailable and untouched by their mothers' deaths. Their mothers died alone. Ultimately, one must believe that this inability to recall or forgive must cost these daughters something in terms of their own completion.

It is apparent, then, that the history of the relationship does not necessarily determine what role daughters will play in the final passing. But what is striking in all these stories is how important the mother-daughter relationship was and continued to be to the daughter. How much the great majority of the daughters wanted to be there for their mothers, to help make their deaths as easy as possible, for their mothers and for themselves, how glad they were to have a chance to say good-bye, or how much they regretted not having the chance to say their final words.

Ultimately, peace comes with acceptance. "We did the best we could in our role of mother and daughter, in living out and through a relationship formed a lifetime ago." In all of the situations, the intensity of feelings—whether of great love and admiration or intense anger and disappointment—all come into play at the end along with everything we were, are, and would like to become.

REFERENCES

1. S. de Beauvoir, *A Very Easy Death,* Pantheon Books, New York, 1965.
2. M. S. Moss and S. Z. Moss, *The Final Transition,* Baywood, Amityville, New York, 1995.

CHAPTER 3

What Death Triggers

> The last formal task of an adult child toward his or her parent is
> to cope with the death of the parent [1, p. 108].

When my mother died, I was old enough to look into the mirror and see her face. It was a double loss: she was gone and the mirror, reaffirming our connection, showed me the inevitability of my own death. I was grieving her death and mine simultaneously.

Her loss took away my last chance to pretend, even for a moment, that I was still a child. Terry Tempest Williams wrote similarly in *Refuge* when she acknowledged that with the death of her mother, she could no longer feel that she was a child, with all that implied in terms of nurturing, love, and history [2, p. 202]. Not only did my mother's death remind me I would be forever the grown-up, but it took away the one person who was unfailingly interested in my daughter and the person with whom I could share what was happening and who was always happy to listen, no matter how trivial my story. There were other losses, too: my history and the fantasy that I might still change the script, make things come out right, be the perfect daughter.

The extent of my loss, then, had to do not only with my mother's absence, but also my relationship to myself. Stephenson writes of two major categories of grief: "reactive," in which the death represents the loss of a loved one upon whom the individual placed a great deal of importance, and "existential," in which the person is forced to look at her own death. Almost all grieving, he maintains, involves elements of both reactive and existential grief [3, p. 126]. While the daughter grieves the loss, she also realizes that what is being experienced is a part of life, and that all life, even one's own, ends in death.

So a mother's death is really a two-pronged trigger, on the one hand, it reminds us at once of all that has been lost, never to be retrieved, and it also puts an end to any vestiges of the illusion that we will live indefinitely. This chapter focuses on these two distinct but closely connected losses, as well as the feelings that attend them. Guilt, another deeply felt aspect death often triggers, gets its own chapter. Though connected to grief, guilt is an offshoot that sometimes distracts from loss and sometimes intensifies feelings of grief.

GRIEF FOR THE LOSS OF A MOTHER
AND WHAT IT MEANS

The grief over their mothers' deaths expressed by the women I spoke with was sometimes pure and sometimes mixed with relief, either because the mother had been such a burden, the relationship so conflicted, or because the mother was suffering so. Although there were those daughters whose relief was unmitigated by any feelings of sorrow (because the daughter found her mother perpetually critical or dissatisfied), those daughters were the exception.

Stephenson cautions that it is essential to understand first what the death means to those grieving before one can begin to understand what the grief means [3, p. 129]. Yet many of the daughters, when asked, could not easily articulate the specific reasons for their own grief. At first many responded, even though close to tears, almost automatically, "I loved my mother." When pushed, they came up with specific, but rather pat responses: "I can't call her on the phone." "I have no one to bring flowers on Mother's Day." Those women seemed to have made the automatic association: mother dies, daughter feels sorrow. They didn't tend to think in greater detail about why they were feeling the way they did. It is significant to note that, by and large, these daughters were often the ones who remained stuck in their grief long after others who could attach specific reasons for their grief and identify some of what their mothers' deaths would change in their lives. The latter group was more readily able to accommodate the loss.

What, exactly, do middle-age women grieve when their mothers die? I, for one, recognized that part of my grief was a kind of generalized sadness that I no longer had a mother. She had been a reference point for fifty-seven years and now she was gone, at least physically. And there were specific things I would miss. I would miss the way we each reaffirmed each other's existence; I'd miss knowing that no matter what, there was one person who would always remember my birthday. I would miss knowing where she was, worrying about whether she was all right, and sharing the memories only she and I could. I would miss the chance to learn more about my life and hers, and even miss the immature part of me that liked to push her buttons, just a little.

Some of what I knew I would miss seems almost too insignificant to mention. I had wanted a photograph of the three generations of women; I lined up a photographer friend to take the photo as soon as my daughter came home from school. When I knew my mother was dying, one of my first thoughts was, "Now we'll never have that picture." I'd miss her telling me my coat needed brushing, my nylons were the wrong shade, and I needed to have my hair cut. Even if I bristled, I respected her opinions—she was usually right.

Recognizing the complexity of my own feelings, I was intensely curious to learn what other women thought about when they talked about their grief over their mothers' deaths. Many could articulate reasons. One of the most universal sentiments among those I interviewed was their grief over no longer having the "key player" in their childhood. This is a common reaction. Moss writes about the grieving person's attempt to recapture the essence of the relationship with the deceased, to dwell on past events and feelings in a life review. The parent who died is recalled in part as the parent of early childhood. Recollections are tinged with grief over unfulfilled wishes and opportunities. While mourning the loss of parents, one also mourns the loss of the family of origin in which they played a central part. "The child in us receives the ultimate blow, our parent is dead, and only the image remains" [1, p. 109].

Ella, recalling her mother, corroborates this sentiment: "I remember with both sadness and joy what a good mother she was, how she did everything she could for me. I remember the family dinners and trips, the sense that we were a unit apart from the rest of the world. I had a happy childhood and much of that is because of my mother." She marvels at the fact that her mother never referred to her mistakes, even when she could have easily reminded me, or said "I told you so." Simone de Beauvoir also looked backwards when her mother was dying: "Time vanished behind those who leave this world, and the older I get the more my past years draw together. The *Maman* darling of the days when I was ten can no longer be told from the inimical woman who oppressed my adolescence; I wept for them both when I wept for my old mother" [4, p. 103].

The daughters often mentioned details from childhood and the security they remembered. Except for the angriest, all the women I talked to could identify some form of comfort they would miss. Even Madeline, whose initial response to her mother's death was one of relief because her mother had been such a burden, found herself saying about a week later, "I miss my mommy. The adult me was not missing her, but missing whatever *mother* meant. I was alone, now, and was, in fact, abandoned."

All those who described their mothers as their chief advocates and cheerleaders said they would miss that unquestioning support. Helena says that her mother always let her know how much she liked her. "She would tell me endlessly and would call me to tell me how much she missed me. My mother was so affirming, especially the last few years; nobody gives you unconditional love except your mother." What Jean missed most about her mother is her "unbridled enthusiasm for me—never again will I know that energy and enthusiasm directed specifically at me. When she died, I lost my cheerleader."

Simply the chance to share their day or their thoughts with their mothers was important, often more so than the daughters had realized. Beverly mentioned missing the opportunity to call and say, "Guess what I did today?" and find someone on the other end who really wanted to know, someone to trade ideas with and give feedback. Jasmine, whose mother lived with her, just liked being able to go to her room and say "whatever." Joan found it strange no longer having her mother to talk to, and acknowledged that her mother, right up until her death, continued to give her opinions and her advice even though she lived 3,000 miles away. "Now, all of a sudden, no more phone calls."

Many women mentioned the hole their mothers' deaths would leave in their everyday lives, ranging from phone calls, lunches, or a warm hug to shared reminiscences and a chance to remember one another with little gifts. These daughters had established small rituals, and their mothers' absence created a kind of disequilibrium. Teri used to call her mother every Thursday and said that after her mother died, she would sometimes call and just let the phone ring.

Jorrie always visited her mother on Sunday; for several months, she wandered around lost on Sunday afternoons. I used to call my mother every morning before she left for lunch. I didn't always want to, but the habit quickly became ingrained.

Funny how important these calls, these check-ins became; it is especially ironic because most of us thought we were only doing it for our mothers. It came as a shock to discover we, also, missed the ritual.

QUIET

My mother is dead; phone disconnected.
I know the dead hover
but she is not listening any more.

Her perfume is still in the house,
her engagement ring in my drawer, but
my mother is dead; phone disconnected.

From the East I hear she might be reborn as egret or dove,
rise up and dance when the moshiach comes
but she is not listening any more.

Her decomposing flesh enriches the soil,
softens the lilac in Addas Israel cemetery, but
my mother is dead; phone disconnected.

She left her history—books of writing, photos, grandchildren;
her advice troubles my sleep
but she is not listening anymore.

In the mirror, no image,
at Thanksgiving, no gravy,
My mother is dead; her phone disconnected,
and she is not listening any more.

Mother is dead; phone disconnected, no forwarding number.
They say the dead's spirit and cells are everywhere
but she, who listened, is not listening any more.

Diane Sher Lutovich

In some cases, the mother was the last connection with the parental home, and very often the focal point for siblings and other relatives. Sukie remembered how important family was to her mother and how she loved to host family gatherings; she would miss that. A mother's home also promised there would always be somewhere where "they have to take you in," something several of the women discovered; Ella and Patti, as well as others, mentioned going home after their divorces, and their mothers were there to support, help, and encourage them.

With her mother gone, Marcia feared that all connection with her extended family would be lost as well. When Marcia was sixteen, her mother married a man with three children, the ages of Marcia and her siblings. Because they were never really integrated into one family, Marcia's mother was the hub around whom the children rotated.

Willa missed being able to take care of her mother, to take her on trips, and to do some role reversing. It was her chance to say to the world, "I was part of something before this life in which you know me only the way I am now." I, too, remember with great fondness the outings, lunches in particular, that gave my mother and me the chance to take pleasure in the connection and the opportunity to affirm "We are here, together." Not your small Greek village, but it would do.

Barbara grieved for the lost possibility of proving to her mother, "I can do it." She had had a difficult relationship with her mother and felt that she never lived up to her mother's expectations for her, chiefly marrying some "alpha male who would join with me in making a family for my mother. That would have pleased her."

Ironically, several women missed being able to talk to their mothers about their remodeling projects—the ones financed with money they inherited from their mothers. (Many of these projects involved kitchens, interestingly enough.) They wanted their mothers' advice and, as Helena said, "mother's decisiveness." She adds she would have been on the phone every day with her mother, discussing colors, textures, and so on.

The women also talked about more abstract losses. Rachel found her grief to be more generalized and intense than she had imagined it would be. Though she had not had a happy relationship with her mother, she says that upon seeing her mother's body, "I felt such a strong connection to the body of my mother through the umbilical cord—as metaphor—and it had been cut. It was just remarkable. I had a feeling that something was missing . . . a feeling that something had been cut off and died." (This is a feeling Simone de Beauvoir also writes about.) Rachel adds, "I had the feeling of being in the womb and adored—a very strong feeling and [that was] part of the loss." Many times right after her mother died, she said, she felt like a little child. There were many moments when all of a sudden "I'd feel like crying, maybe a longing for togetherness with the mother that I really never had."

Joanne was also surprised at both her sense of the passing years and the feeling the umbilical cord had been severed. She describes feeling very isolated; as long as her mother was alive, if she ever needed anything, her mother would be there. Since her mother's death, she says, "I feel like a homeless person—a part of me is lost, a part I didn't even know was there, the connection."

There are other losses as well. Sandra stated, "My mother took the record of my life with her when she died." She went on to say that "I'm carrying the whole history of my family, but there is no one to tell it to." Koru misses the "sense of balance, security, place, and comfort" she derived from taking care of her mother. Vivian, who successfully ran a business and raised three children, longed for the chance to have "someone to push against."

So many of the feelings expressed in the interviews—loss, finality, childhood ended—are summed up in this poem by Carolyn Miller.

CLEANING

First I moved all the papers out of the kitchen,
the greeting cards and letters and the lists
written in my mother's beautiful, shaky
hand. I moved stacks of magazines and bills
and piles of notices from the Readers' Digest
Sweepstakes off the brown Formica breakfast table,
and took cups and glasses full of ballpoint pens, bobby pins,
thumbtacks, razor blades, old keys, and coins
off the wavy linoleum counter, and old phone books
and piles of papers with names and telephone numbers
and put everything beside the boxes and baskets
of photographs and the leaning towers
of *Readers' Digests* and Southern Baptist bulletins
and the dying begonias in the sunroom. Then
I took out the vacuum cleaner

and went through the house, sweeping up
the dust that layered everything in the home
of a woman who believed that dust was sinful,
cleaning under the bed and pulling out balled-up socks,
dusting the venetian blinds and sucking up dead
leaves and cobwebs and fallen plaster, and I cleaned
the bathtub and the toilet, working as fast I could
without stopping, sweating and breathing hard.
Then I took the towels off the recliner and the worn sofa,
I stripped the sheets off the bed and the cases
off the pillows, and I sorted through the piles of dirty clothes
and I washed the socks and pajamas and underwear,
using the blue Cheer in the plastic container. Then
I dried everything in the failing Maytag and
folded the warm clothes. Next I went through the house
moving the ugliest vases and teapots and bowls
and ceramic statues downstairs to the basement,
rearranging and grouping and adjusting, trying
to get it all back to the way it was when I was a child,
when my mother was young and strong, and finally I went outside
and picked up the shingles that had blown off the roof
and pulled up some of the weeds that had invaded
the yard and straightened the fallen flowerpots
and put the rusting lawn chair back where it was
when my mother sat and watched the birds at twilight.
And then, the last day of my stay almost over,
I walked out into the woods, where I hadn't gone
until now, though they were filled with blooming dogwood
and redbud and a soft gray-brown multiplicity of branches,
and even though the path had disappeared,
I walked through the dry layer of oak leaves
that covered the floor of the woods to my old place,
the little clearing above the limestone cave
that, long ago, at just this time of year,
I had decorated as an Easter surprise for my mother.
Now there was no nest of colored eggs,
or crepe paper streamers in the trees, and no Easter bunnies
in the grass, but as though they had been waiting
all this time, small bouquets of Johnny-jump-ups
were blossoming among the dead leaves. I sat,
looking at the flooded valley far below, in the woods
where I had spent long days
climbing rocks and dreaming on the moss,
and I said to myself: *This is not my home anymore* [5].

GRIEF FOR OURSELVES

The death of a mother removes a psychological buffer against one's own death. As long as the parent is alive, the child can feel protected, since the parent, by all rational order, is expected to die first. After one's parents' deaths, particularly when one is already well into middle age, it is much harder to deny one's own mortality. In fact, it is a red flag—there is more time behind than ahead.

This awareness can engender its own grief, Stephenson's "existential grief." The lost relationship may have served as the individual's defense against death. After her mother died, Meg said, she was suddenly conscious of the limited time she had left to come into her own and of the fact that she is "sitting in the front-line generation." With both parents dead "that makes you the next." Penny talked about her mother's death putting her into another life phase. "It was a process of maturation, forcing me to integrate sorrow and loss." Sue, like many others, said she keeps looking around for "the others" who would go before her, and noted, with some chagrin, there were none.

According to Kowalski, the child, no matter how old he or she might be, becomes an orphan when the second parent dies [6, p. 129]. (Of the women I spoke with, the death of the mother represented the loss of the second parent in the majority of cases.) Beverly stated that not only did she feel like an orphan, but that she got "boosted up a generational level." Virtually all the daughters were keenly aware of what this means in terms of their own mortality. Marcia found that the physical symptoms that had bothered her, such as shortness of breath, became much more acute after her mother died; within the first week after her mother's death, she made an appointment for a complete physical exam.

THINKING AHEAD

As if one's own mortality were not enough to contemplate, grieving daughters may also feel, at least on an unconscious level, that they are likely to age and die the way their mothers did. This seems to be true both for the cause of death as well as the individual's reaction to dying. This recognition is much harder to discount when the survivor is the same gender as the deceased. With the greater involvement and intensity of lengthier parent-child relationships, it is hardly surprising that middle-age daughters look to the way their mothers died, either in hope or fear of emulating them. When the mother's death was inspiring, it offers her daughter hope that she, too, will die with fortitude and courage. There is the other side as well: If her mother set a good example, a daughter may not live up to it. On the other hand, if the mother died angrily and bitterly, shouting over and over "I refuse to die," as Vivian's did, there is the fear of repeating the trauma, but also the challenge of surmounting it.

Helena is one of those who wants to emulate her mother. She says that her mother had no thought for herself, no self-pity, no self-absorption—she was only thinking about what she could give to others. "She would open up; she was just precious." Her mother talked about her dying, saying that she was looking forward to it and found the whole experience very interesting. She had a strong feeling that she would see people she had known. "She said to me, 'It won't be easy to say good-bye to you but I know that I'm going to a better place.'" And she kept quoting a poem she had learned as a child.

Helena adds that she was astonished at how much control her mother had, "that she could hold out until my husband got there— she had told him . . . she would wait. During the time she was dying, I thought about my own death—in terms of what a right way might be—to live with our own death totally in front of us. You'd wish for that."

I, too, see my own mother as a wonderful role model. She had made all the arrangements in advance with her very understanding physician, and as soon as she was told she was dying, she announced she was ready. When my former husband visited, she was able to tell him how sorry she was that he and I had not been able to make a go of our marriage, but how glad she was that we had each found others to care about. And when my long-time partner came to see her, she told him how glad she was that I had him to take care of me. Imagine, dying at ninety-two and still wanting to make sure your fifty-seven-year-old daughter is all right. I only hope that I will do half as well: making my plans so my daughter will be spared those very tough decisions, feeling that I am ready, and leaving everyone with a final, and very real message of love.

RANGE OF RESPONSES

There are many factors that contribute to how a daughter responds to her mother's death, actual or impending. Of those I talked with some were devastated and felt they would never get over the loss. Others felt sorrow, but took comfort in knowing they had done what they could for their mothers' final days and gave themselves time to absorb the loss and move on. Some continued on with their lives in the same way, while others changed their priorities. Many found the loss spurred them to think more carefully about how they wanted to spend the rest of their lives; what plans they needed to make for their own well-being; how they would respond to their own grown children; and what changes they'd like to make in family dynamics.

In cases where the deaths were quite recent, it was not possible to know about the daughters' long-term reactions. Other deaths, however, had taken place as long as ten years earlier and while most of the women in these cases had comfortably incorporated the loss, a few seemed to continue to suffer. Again, with the exception of those women who felt unmitigated relief at their mothers' death, there is a range of reactions from "I'll miss her but I'm mostly grateful she went peacefully" to "I feel as if the hole left by her death will last forever. She was my best listener, my best friend." From "now I am finally free of that family" to "I must do everything I can to keep the family together."

Kalish found that some people recover from the death of another within the expected time and with minimal vestiges of disrupted behavior; for others, time seems of little use as a remedy and personal behavior remains disrupted [7, p. 196].

Jasmine was an only child who said she was very close to her mother. For twenty-two years, they lived only seven minutes from one another. Two years before she died, Jasmine's mother started "going downhill," and asked her daughter "What good am I to you?" Her daughter replied that simply her being there was enough. Two years after her mother's death, Jasmine still felt it was a terrible loss, that it would have been easier if "we had not been living the same city where we could see each other every day." This observation is supported by C. M. Parkes who postulates another set of factors that contribute to grief, including the magnitude of the transition [8, p. 305]. Women whose mothers were living with them or who saw them every day, as Jasmine did, seemed to grieve more intensely than those who had a less integrated connection. But, of course, it is also safe to say that in all probability their mothers were living with them because they had a particular bond.

Jasmine did not say what made her mother so important in her life, only that she was. She stands in contrast to others like Nancy and Lana, who felt their mothers' deaths were not a "big deal."

Most of the daughters I spoke with would fit somewhere in the middle of this continuum. These include Patti, who felt she had been a good daughter and had done all she could to make her mother's last days comfortable. One reason Patti felt that she did not feel any paralyzing grief when her mother died was that she spent more time with her mother in the five weeks before she died than she had in many years. She also credits her recent training in counseling in helping her prepare.

She was with her mother when the physician told her that he didn't think she should pursue extraordinary measures to prolong her life. Patti recognized that what she had to do was the hardest thing—to just be there with her mother. Something she had never done before but knew would give the most comfort was recounting all the wonderful times with her mother and telling her how much "I loved her and how much I would miss her." She also thinks it helped that, "We took care of the difference between us indirectly. I'm not even sure she ever wanted it to be a spoken thing. I did end up telling her she had done a wonderful job and how much I appreciated her. I told her things I didn't even believe. Why not? If this were me, what would I want to hear? And I just made up wonderful tales."

She says that she hasn't experienced any period of depression and anxiety about her mother's death. And though that sometimes worries her, she reminds herself, "I was prepared."

CONTRIBUTING FACTORS

What makes the difference in a daughter's ability to accept and mourn the death of her mother and move on with her life? Researchers have put forth many theories about the influences that come into play in determining a survivor's response to a significant loss. Kastenbaum refers to Sanders' findings that suggest the type of person seems to be more important than other factors [9, p. 234]. That is, how the individual tends to cope with stress in his or her life in general proved to be more closely related to bereavement outcome twenty-four months later than the specific nature of bereavement (child, parent, or spouse). These findings were based on Sanders' interviews with participants right after the death of a loved one and again between eighteen and twenty-four months later.

Sanders identified four types of bereavement patterns: Disturbed, Depressed/High-Grief, Denial, and Normal/Grief-Controlled, that is, people who were able to express their feelings and move ahead with their lives. She notes that study participants showed a characteristic pattern of response to grief over time. Some people, for example, showed a general pattern of trying to maintain a "stiff upper lip," covering up any signs of distress. Most interesting, Sanders found that, contrary to expectations, those who used the denial coping strategies did not break down for failure to talk about their grief. In fact, most of the "stiff upper lippers" had their grief responses under reasonable control at the time of the initial interview and two years later [10].

The "Normals" showed reductions in the level of grief intensity over the two-year period while most of the people in the "Disturbed" group remained almost as anxious as they had been soon after the death. The "Depressed" had made some progress after two years, but were also experiencing symptoms usually associated with acute grief; many of these were facing continued or new forms of stress that made it particularly difficult for them to work through their grief.

Based on these observations, Kastenbaum draws another conclusion, one separate from the impact of one's general coping style. He believes that it can be a mistake to set any kind of time for grief or expect all people to be at a certain level of recovery by a particular time [9, p. 234].

Andrew E. Scharlach found two factors to be primary contributors to the extent of both initial and residual grief reactions: the expectation of a parent's death and the independence of the daughter [11, p. 310]. For the most part, those women who had prepared for their mothers' deaths were more able to move through their grief without major trauma. Among the women I interviewed, all except one (whose mother died in a plane crash) had some reason to be prepared for their mothers' deaths—either because their mothers were very old or because they had a terminal illness. Sometimes the actual death trajectory was fast, but still there were clues—advanced age, if nothing else—although in many cases, including my own, the daughter chose not to see the imminence of death. A part of this anticipatory grief is just recognizing the situation, which can allow for anticipatory coping, including grieving in advance for what will be lost.

Another way to anticipate is becoming familiar with the process—both for the dying person and the survivors. Many of the women who were truly present for their mothers as they were dying talked about the reading they did that allowed them to be honest, open, and available during this time. Helena said the information she got from hospice was extremely helpful, and others, such as Patti, did their own research. They knew what to expect and were prepared. A list of some of the books daughters found helpful are listed in Suggested Reading, page 143.

Anticipatory grief work can include recognizing your own feelings about a parent's approaching death, as well as thinking about and even writing down those feelings. According to some grief counselors, acknowledging feelings and facing the reality of the impending death makes it easier to accept when it actually occurs.

Preparation for a parent's death also offers a chance to bring a sense of closure to the relationship, maybe ending a long-lasting feud, making promises or apologies, expressing love, gratitude, remorse, and other emotions. Many of the daughters did this, but most did so indirectly. Many daughters wanted to talk frankly with their mothers but, because feelings were not talked about in their family, they were afraid to do so. So they, like Patti, took care of the differences indirectly, by simply being present, talking about the lives they had shared, and having loving intentions.

Another consistent factor in the impact of a parent's death, Scharlach found, was the extent to which the "children" depended on the deceased for emotional support and approval: the greater the need, the greater the difficulty when the parent died [11, p. 310]. Apparently, dependency and need for parental approval were more salient predictors of distress following a parent's death than were other characteristics usually considered to be signs of anxious attachment. Bleckner found, as quoted by Scharlach, that healthy adult parent-child relationships are presumed to reflect "filial maturity," the ability to attain an adult-adult relationship with one's parent where neither parent nor child assumes the dominant role.

My interviews corroborated Scharlach's findings. The women I talked with who suffered intensely at their mothers' death did appear to be in some way dependent on their mothers. These are the women who had continued to regard their mothers as the primary source of emotional validation and support. For example, Natalie, even though she knew the path of her life differed from the one her mother would have chosen for her, still wanted her mother to at least pay lip service to the fact that her daughter had lived a good life and that she approved of her daughter's choices. Still waiting for that approval, Natalie took a long time to get over the loss she felt when her mother died. Barbara, too, was still depending on, or at least hoping for, her mother's approval at the time her mother died. She felt that once "I was able to accomplish what she expected me to," her mother would be happy with her. Barbara found it difficult to accept her mother's dying before she achieved this goal.

MOURNING

Women mourn differently from men. According to Robbins, women's development points toward a history of human attachment that stresses continuity and reconfiguration rather than displacement and separation, the typical mourning pattern of men [12, p. 145]. In other words, women seek a way to preserve and continue a relationship with the deceased, while men distance themselves from the loss and seek a replacement. One need only look at how much more quickly men tend to remarry—the difference is not only demographics.

It would be logical to assume, then, that women's patterns of attachment may show a different response to loss and offer a different metaphor of assimilation and growth. It takes into account that the relationship continues, which for most women it does. Many women talked about the daily conversations they had with their deceased mothers. Because of their need for continuity, women, rather than "simply getting on with their lives," need to look for ways to mend the hole left by the death and find a way to restore what has been torn, that is, the story of themselves in relation to their mothers. (More on this in Chapter 7, "Holding On and Moving Forward.")

As stated earlier and stressed in much of the research, the mourning process is not linear. The grief goes away and comes back. I was always surprised, during the first year after my mother died, and even now occasionally (over 4 years later), to be driving or walking and the slightest whisper would make me think of her and the tears would come. It could be the sight of an old woman, it could be songs she loved, or it could be just a free-floating memory, one that I couldn't attach to anything. Many women speak of the same phenomena, which are completely normal. Parkes, among others, calls them "pangs" [8, p. 39]. Pangs of grief begin within a few hours or days of bereavement and usually reach a peak of severity within five to fourteen days. They certainly become less frequent over time, but I'm still astonished when seemingly out of the blue, I think of my mother. These days, the images are less likely to evoke deep sadness. Still, they are almost always accompanied by a wish that she were still alive, or that she had had a happier life, or that I had been a different, better daughter. I don't try to distract myself when these images and thoughts occur. They don't last long; they allow me to "touch" her. My mind quickly enough returns to where it should be.

Along with these "pangs" are the anniversary reactions of which many of the daughters spoke. They were apt to experience a deep sadness on their mothers' birthdays, the anniversaries of their deaths, or even on their own birthdays. Several of the women I spoke with use the occasion to honor their mothers, rather than see them only as occasions for grieving. Ama plants flowers. Georgia always bakes cookies on her mother's birthday and brings them to the residence where her mother lived. She puts them out with a note "from my mother." It is a gesture Georgia finds more helpful than going to the cemetery, but others, including Joanne, feel right going to visit their mothers' graves on the anniversary. She says she gives her mother an update and leaves a flower from one of her mother's plants.

Women found many ways to comfort themselves in the short term and when confronted with the "pangs" of anniversary reactions. These are described in more detail in Chapter 6.

PROBLEMATIC GRIEF

Sometimes grievers become stuck and are unable to resolve and complete their mourning in a predictable way. Stephenson says that "it is probably safe to assume that a lack of recognition of a significant loss, an extreme reaction far in excess of normative cultural expectations, and a lack of movement through the grief process can be considered to indicate difficulty in resolving the loss, something we label exceptional grief" [3, p. 151]. Others, too, found the process of mourning will often go awry. Certainly Willa and Jasmine fit this pattern. Years after their mothers died, they cried at the mention of them, still had trouble sleeping, had made a shrine of their belongings, and continued to blame themselves for not being better daughters. These "stuck" daughters often experience guilt, as well as grief.

Frozen grief, on the other hand, is a lack of recognition of the significant loss, as described by Robbins, which can arise in difficult relationships. This cuts off a woman's feelings, alienating her both from her mother's memory and from her own female self. Robbins argues that women unable to grieve need to reconnect with their memories of their mothers, something that can only be accomplished by recognizing their mothers in the context in which they lived. Otherwise, Robbins predicts, such women will continue to live with a suppressed rage, "devouring others through emotional manipulation and herself through depression" [12, p. 265].

After a period of time, extreme reactions may surface in a variety of clinical symptoms, including a painful response when the mother is mentioned, a realization of unresolved grief and unaccountable depression, or the emergence of medical symptoms on the anniversary of the loss.

Kowalski mentions another kind of problematic grief that he refers to as "partial grief" [6, p. 194], which can accompany a long period of dying often accompanied by the mother's no longer recognizing her daughter. Virginia is one of the daughters who was witness to a prolonged and troublesome death. She remembers her mother "was not doing well" by the time she was seventy-five. Virginia and her husband found her a house close to theirs and encouraged her to move. "I instigated the move because I wanted her to be near." But once she moved in, Virginia remembers, her mother found it very difficult to make a life for herself. She kept saying "I don't know what's wrong." Looking back, Virginia realizes that it was the start of her Alzheimer's, which began to surface soon afterward. While taking care of her granddaughter, she called the police to get Virginia and her husband out of the theater because their child was not going to sleep. Another time, her mother went out to the store and couldn't find her way home. Virginia says, "It was such a strange thing; we didn't know anything about Alzheimer's and since she didn't get lost again, we put it out of our minds." But then her mother started letting pots burn on the stove and once she was found walking along the freeway in the middle of the night. When she had hip surgery and needed an attendant, she would fight with anyone hired to stay with her.

Finally, she went into a nursing home. "At that time she no longer knew where or who she was, so it was no longer stressful for either of us." Virginia said, "The whole thing was just ghastly. I don't know how I survived it. There were times before she was in the nursing home I would shut the phone off because she'd call at any hour." By the time her mother no longer recognized her, Virginia felt her mother's life "was over," even though her mother lived another year.

These prolonged and helpless situations produce their own kind of grief and depression in the family members who care for ailing mothers. In addition to losing a mother and watching her suffer under the care of someone else, these daughters have to deal with the fact that they look forward to their mothers' deaths, knowing it is right for their mothers to die. (In fact, one daughter tried to end her mother's misery herself. She feels guilty only because she failed in her attempts.) Although it is rarely mentioned, daughters in these situations frequently wish for their mothers' release and the chance to regain their own lives. This is an increasing problem. Now that the aged and infirm are physically so well cared for, they can no longer count on a quick release through pneumonia or similar opportunistic diseases.

SUMMING UP

When a daughter loses her mother, especially when she's been a part of her daughter's life for five decades or more, a whole range of feelings are set into motion. First is grief that the mother is gone and all that her absence represents: from loss of one's best cheerleader to the last connection to childhood. This loss, or the memories of it, rarely go away completely. In fact, medical professionals report that frequently a dying patient's last words are about his or her parents, even though those parents might be dead fifty years or more. What touches us first is often what touches us last.

Then there is grief for the self—the recognition of being "next in line." So many women had been able to deny their own mortality as long as their mothers lived. Was it that the mother of childhood would protect them? Or was it some belief of the daughter's that it wasn't her turn yet—as long as her mother was alive?

A mother's death embodies many kinds of losses and elicits many responses to these losses. It helps a mourner move through her grief when she can see clearly and understand what she has lost. Whether it is the final chance to prove herself, her mother's companionship, or just having a mother—the more you know about what you have lost, the easier it is to confront and resolve it. This takes time. And because women grieve differently than men, they must have the time and space to go through the process in their own way.

Along with this awareness, it is also important to recognize the variety of factors that make it harder or easier to cope with the loss of a mother. Personality traits come into play and how you respond to life problems in general influences your reaction. Learn about yourself. Cut yourself some slack. There are reasons you feel the way you do. If your mother's death brings up fears of your own end, pay attention to how she died. You might want to start now to think about how you want to be when you are dying and what changes you will have to make to emulate her grace or avoid her fear and anger.

It is also important to remember that grief is not linear. You will be feeling fine when out of nowhere you will be plunged back into a sense of your loss or recognition of your own aging. Accept these changes. They will be with you for a long time, maybe forever.

Regardless of the circumstance, the most fortunate daughters seem to be those who are open to feeling the loss, both for what was and what could never be.

REFERENCES

1. M. S. Moss and S. Z. Moss, *The Final Transition*, Baywood, Amityville, New York, 1995.
2. T. T. Williams, *Refuge, An Unnatural History of Family and Place*, Vintage Books, New York, 1992.
3. J. S. Stephenson, *Death, Grief, and Mourning: Individual and Social Realities*, The Free Press, New York, 1985.
4. S. de Beauvoir, *A Very Easy Death*, Pantheon Books, New York, 1965.
5. C. Miller, *Cleaning* (poem), unpublished, used by permission of the author.

6. N. C. Kowalski, Anticipating the Death of an Elderly Parent, in *Loss and Anticipatory Grief,* Therese A. Rando (ed.), Lexington Books, Lexington, Massachusetts, 1986.
7. R. A. Kalish, *Death, Grief, and Caring Relationships,* Brooks/Cole, Monterey, California, 1985.
8. C. M. Parkes and J. Steven-Hind (eds.), *The Place of Attachment in Human Behavior, Postulated Causes of Chronic Grief and Their Preventive Implications,* Basic Books, New York, 1982.
9. R. Kastenbaum, *Death, Society and Human Experience,* The C. V. Mosby Company, St. Louis, Missouri, 1981.
10. C. M. Sanders, Unpublished doctoral dissertation, University of South Florida, 1977.
11. A. W. Scharlach, Factors Associated with Filial Grief Following the Death of an Elderly Parent, *American Journal of Orthopsychiatry, 61*:2, April 1991.
12. M. A. Robbins, *Midlife Women and Death of Mother: A Study of Psycho-historical and Spiritual Transformation,* Peter Lang, New York, 1990.

CHAPTER 4
Guilty or Not

> Since you never do all you might for anyone—not even within the arguable limits that you have set yourself—you have plenty of room left for self-reproach. With regard to *Maman*, we were above all guilty, these last years, of carelessness, omission and abstention [1, p. 94].

When my father died shortly before my eighteenth birthday, I felt grief, but no guilt. When my mother died almost forty years later, I had a whole laundry list of guilts. I felt guilty over little things—all the times I was late picking her up—and the big things—moving away from her when she needed me most. In my view, my father inhabited and left a world separate from mine, whereas I could identify with my mother completely. In some way, I felt responsible for her, and consequently could find so many ways in which I let her down.

A mother's death is the perfect breeding ground for guilt. When you start with a mother who is sad, lonely, and unfulfilled, as many in my mother's generation were, then add the very tight connection between mother and daughter, throw in a dash (or more) of tension during adolescence, let sit in a dark place for many decades and then finish with the mother's death, it is the rare daughter who is not susceptible to at least a few pangs of guilt.

It is not surprising, then, that the subject of guilt came up repeatedly when daughters talked about their mothers. In fact, the only daughters interviewed who did not mention the word guilt were the extremes: those who had no tender memories, or those whose memories were particularly positive. In this latter group are women who remembered their relationships with their mothers as ones based on mutual respect, who accepted themselves and their mothers as people who did their best under the circumstances of their lives. And of that group, the even more fortunate (and guiltless), were told often by their mothers what wonderful daughters they were.

Like myself, however, most daughters noted myriad guilts, big and small: their mothers had lived such sad lives, which their daughters couldn't make better; they had disappointed their mothers when they moved away or in how they chose to live their lives; they were not sufficiently sacrificing or attentive when their mothers were sick; or they weren't with them when they were dying.

Many daughters who were particularly guilt prone appeared to be tied to their mothers in a special way, either by setting unreasonable expectations for themselves or by taking on those defined for them by their mothers. Even if mothers did not set out to foster guilt, they communicated the kinds of messages that would make their already emotionally involved daughters feel it. For example, Sarah still remembered how she had to cut short her mother's weeping about her father's affair because she had to go to cheerleading practice, only to weep herself, all through practice. Sarah, like many others, was asked to share the pain of her mother's life and felt guilty because she could do nothing to make it better. This life-long conditioning often takes its greatest toll after a mother's death.

Another factor contributing to a daughter's feelings of guilt may be the lack of support and appreciation for her expressions of love and efforts to care for her mother. Many unhappy aging mothers let their caretaking daughters know they aren't doing enough, or they're doing it too reluctantly, or they lack a generosity of spirit. One woman I know who is devoting herself to her mother's final years said that her mother always reminds her that she is acting out of obligation rather than desire. This daughter can't argue the point, but she has a strong urge to say, "So what? I'm doing it."

Finding appropriate living situations in nursing homes or similar facilities for incapacitated mothers is a decision daughters must often make and often yet another reason for guilt. The fact that she may have no choice is not always enough to assuage a daughter's guilt. According to N. Claire Kowalski, guilt feelings often arise from the notion that families are supposed to take care of their own. That notion arose, however, when the elderly did not require extended care. Lingering inability to care for oneself was a rare phenomenon, unlike presently [2, p. 196].

Other regrets or guilts described by daughters would cause mothers who have been totally ignored or even abandoned to shake their heads in amazement. For example, many daughters strongly regretted their inability to have more physical contact with their mothers. Having grown up in less repressive times, these daughters were more comfortable with their own physicality than were their mothers. Many had been involved in some form of therapy, and had come to put a higher regard on touching and holding. I'm one of those who berated herself, even while my mother was well, for not touching and hugging her more. In retrospect, it's quite possible that this failure to "touch" was not as much a daughter's withholding, but a consequence of a mother's sending a very strong message that "bodies are private." I remember few hugs and kisses after my earliest years that did not seem forced and awkward.

Another regret common among this generation of daughters seems to be their failure to push for more intimacy, more disclosure. Many, while recognizing their mothers' need to be closed off (or their inability to be open), wish they had tried harder to get to know who their mothers really were. Instead, they regret having only had a superficial relationship because they, as daughters, were so careful not to disturb their mothers' self-protectiveness.

REASONS FOR GUILT

Of the reasons daughters gave for feeling guilty, some were logical and some not; some abstract, some specific; some about their own lives, some about their mothers? Because none of those I interviewed were guilty of egregious crimes, the faults and omissions they revealed were usually self-defined: regrets for things done or undone; words spoken or not.

The feeling that one should have done more is pervasive. Anne Rosberger describes one of her clients, about six months after her mother had died, as a woman who clung to the feeling she should have done more for her mother. She was plagued with self-doubt about almost everything including her choice of doctors, treatment, and so on. Even though her relationship with her mother had been a good one, she desperately wanted one more chance to tell her mother how much she loved her and to make up for any arguments they had ever had. She was so overcome with guilt, she doubted she would ever feel happy [3, p. 121].

Natalie described her reaction to her mother's death in terms of the guilt she felt. Natalie reproaches herself mostly for not dropping her psychology practice and moving in with her mother when she was dying and desperately wanted her to. She berates herself for not closing her office and going back to Boston to "be with my mother as long as it took for her to die." Two years after the death, Natalie stated, "I feel so badly—I should have said to hell with it, gone there to be with her—but at the time, I just didn't see how I could do it." She said her guilt is just now starting to ease, but for at least a year she had serious problems sleeping. "I thought about her constantly, mostly a lot of it was regret—she really needed me—I don't feel I did half enough—I desperately felt I didn't do enough."

More than three years after her mother died, Jasmine still felt that "I killed my mother." Her mother, eighty-nine and blind, suffered a stroke. Jasmine knew that her mother wanted no heroic measures and had signed a living will, and yet at the last moment, "I wanted to override her." Finally, she explained, she let the three doctors convince her. "They kept reminding me of what my mother wanted, so I let her go."

Jasmine had been a devoted daughter who stopped by to see her mother every day. She felt so close to her mother that she said, "You can always replace your husband, but not your mother." About her mother's death, she said, "It doesn't seem to help when the doctors remind me that I followed her wishes." She suggested that "maybe part of the grieving process is to blame yourself."

Sarah's deepest regrets also have to do with the way she handled her mother's dying. When her mother started doing frightening things, like wandering into the street, Sarah moved her to a residential center that was highly recommended. Her mother was adamantly opposed to going. "I would not do it if I had it to do again," she said. Sarah was told it would be easier for her mother to make the adjustment if her daughter did not visit for a week, so she didn't—yet another decision she regrets. At first her mother seemed to be adjusting, but then she fell out of her bed and hurt her back.

After that, her mother started acting out and the residence could no longer keep her. Sarah found another living situation and brought her mother there for lunch, to give the administrators the opportunity to see if she was suitable. She was desperate for her mother to "pass." When her mother fell asleep during lunch, Sarah was sure she would not be admitted. Later, her mother started leaning into her "as if she wanted to be cuddled and I left her there. I feel so bad about that." Sarah said that was when doctors discovered her mother had pneumonia. As she was driving her mother to the hospital, her mother said, "there's nothing for me to do but to die," and her daughter told her "you're right." After that, Sarah was unable to stop crying over the hopelessness of her mother's life.

"When you have children, you love them and take care of them. They're a breeze compared to taking care of dying parents," Sarah stated. "The point at which I could no longer make her happy, it was over."

Koru's story is similar. Even after the years of joy and devotion with which she cared for her mother "day by day," Koru blamed herself for her mother's fall. Although her mother had been getting weaker, she rallied enough so they could go to Koru's sister's for Thanksgiving. On the way home, her mother slipped going up the stairs to her apartment and fell backward. Koru said her mother must have thought that she was behind to catch her, but she wasn't.

After that serious fall, her mother declined rapidly. "She was finished," Koru said and speculated that her mother might have just been too tired to recover. Koru felt her mother's death was her fault. "If only I had been there to catch her . . ."

Irene's guilt derives from feeling that what she told her mother might have precipitated her death. Her mother was in the hospital recovering from a heart attack when Irene told her that Mark, the man she had been living with, had moved out. Her mother had been very close to Mark and "so I know she felt bad even though she didn't say anything. I know she wanted me to be with someone. I feel so guilty because maybe my telling her was upsetting enough that it brought on the final heart attack." She admitted that she'll never know for sure.

Sandra's regrets are focused on the fact that she wasn't able "to say to my mother, please come and live with me." She also regrets that "when she was ill, I wasn't able to do more nonverbally—to massage her feet, to hold her hand." The major commitment she made (to take a leave from her job and go to Arizona to take care of her mother for 3 months) does not seem to fill her with the pride and clear conscience one would expect.

Madeline mentioned two significant guilts that she carried: one specific, the other abstract. The first has to do with the death itself. Madeline's son had called to tell her she should come immediately, her mother was dying. She said that at the time, "I felt she had been such a burden, I was so sick of her complaining, I just couldn't make myself go." She said she had a very ambivalent relationship with her mother, but that she ended up feeling guilty that she wasn't with her mother when she died. Taking care of all the funeral arrangements and visiting the grave helped assuage the guilt.

The abstract guilt Madeline had been dealing with much longer was her sense that her mother never wanted her to be "self-sufficient and happy." Madeline, a highly successful attorney with several advanced degrees and a wonderful second marriage, was both. She felt that her mother, who came to this country from Greece, unable to speak English, and married to a man who was away much of the time, was neither self-sufficient nor happy. According to Madeline, she wanted her daughter to live the same kind of life; at least her daughter would need her, feel close to her. As irrational as it might seem, Madeline believes she disappointed her mother by living a positive, fulfilling life. This is not unusual according to Martha Robbins, who found in her study that: "Strong feelings of guilt in the form of abandoning the mother surface if the daughter puts more energy and time in pursuing her own interests in place of caring for the mother" [4, p. 192].

Madeline was one of several daughters who was left feeling extreme grief and guilt—not only for their own losses or their actions toward their mothers, but for the sadness, even tragedy, of their mothers' lives.

PROBLEMATIC GUILT: THREE STORIES

There is no question that guilt interferes with the mourning process. It is a detour on which a daughter can get very lost. As long as she dwells on and berates herself for real or imagined crimes, she is moving away from the true significance of her mother's death—acceptance of the loss and the opportunity for growth.

Among the daughters that I interviewed, I found the nature of their guilt to be of two types: "moral guilt" and "fallible guilt." Those who experienced moral guilt were women whose feelings of guilt seemed to exist independently of what they could or could not provide for their mothers. No matter how large or small the deeds over which they suffered, they felt to an extreme that they could have done more or done it better or differently.

Their stories, however, show that by any reasonable standard, they did not fail to do all they could for their mothers. It has to be something else that is creating these feelings. In some cases, as Martha Robbins discovered, the daughter has not been able to distinguish her own reality from that of her mother and so tries to make up for her mother all that she never had [4, p. 197]. These daughters don't see that they have given themselves an impossible task and their guilt derives from not obtaining it. They can't recognize that it wasn't their job to fix their mothers' lives in the first place.

These women, not conscious of how bound up they were with their mothers' suffering, or of their own need (and inability) to make up to them what they had suffered during their lifetime as well as during their dying, tended to suffer more intensely from guilt than those who had made more of a separation from their mothers.

Women experiencing what I termed fallible guilt, on the other hand, were more realistic in their expectations of themselves and seem to have done a better job at separating the truth of their own lives from that of their mothers'. They, too, could point to specific things they did or failed to do that they feel compromised their mothers' well being. Yet either because of the nature of their actions or, more than likely, because of their own personalities, they were not weighed down with guilt (although they felt it) but able to acknowledge and experience their loss.

Willa, Barbara, and Deborah were all brought up with the sense that they were responsible in some way for their mothers' happiness. While Deborah eventually gained a more realistic sense of her relationship with her mother, Willa and Barbara had trouble moving beyond their sense of failure for not providing for their mothers what the world had failed to give them. After their mothers' deaths, then, instead of grappling with their own life changes and sense of loss (and what it portends in terms of their own deaths), Willa and Barbara focused all their attention on what they did wrong, how their mothers suffered, and how they failed.

More than eight years after her mother's death, Willa can't talk about her without crying. Willa's mother, living in Houston at the time of her stroke, was brought to a hospital near her daughter's home in Milwaukee to convalesce. After her release from the hospital, at Willa's insistence, she moved in with her daughter.

For a year, Willa, who worked full time and had a husband in poor health and three adolescent children at home, tried to accommodate herself and her family to her mother's needs. Because her mother needed continual attending (she was paralyzed from the neck down) Willa hired around-the-clock help. She turned one room of her house into a hospital room. But one attendant after another quit or failed to show up. Willa described it as "a nightmare."

Finally Willa's husband told her he couldn't live that way any longer and so she reluctantly agreed to find her mother a nursing home. She found the best one available. Despite her care, Willa still felt terrible because "I left her in a world of strangers . . . I feel so guilty for not being able to keep her in my home. I was her only familiar face. I loved her so much." In putting her mother in a nursing home, Willa felt that she had created a situation in which her mother was once again deprived of what she deserved.

Willa's mother had come to this country from Sweden as a young woman. Her marriage was one of convenience to a depressed man who was angry most of the time. After he died when Willa was barely six, she remembered her mother being desperate. She had no way to support herself or her daughter. They lived in two rooms above a cleaning store her mother bought with the help of relatives. Even after her mother remarried, her life was little improved. She didn't have to work as hard or live in such mean circumstances, but she didn't love her husband, and her daughter could see how unhappy her mother was.

Willa, like many other daughters, was convinced that at the very least it was her duty to provide her mother a home in which to live her last days. Despite almost losing her family in that year she tried to care for her mother, and despite the fact that she went to see her mother every single day for the two years she was in the nursing facility, Willa still cried and accused herself of not doing enough. "I should have been a more loving daughter, should have been a better daughter. I wish I had been more giving."

Given her life with all of its obligations and pulls, it is hard not to feel Willa did all she could. In her feelings of guilt and grief over her mother's death, she is clearly identifying with the suffering of her mother's life. Willa might also be hiding some other feelings of her own. It is possible that if her mother's life was as miserable as Willa remembered it, her mother may have been unable to give her daughter the nurturing she needed. She might, even if only on some unconscious level, have feelings of disappointment, even anger. Willa, however, doesn't mention her own disappointments—only her mother's. By holding onto her guilt, she may be avoiding dealing directly with her own very difficult losses—as a child and as an adult.

Barbara's mother left on the last boat taking Jews out of Nazi-occupied France. Her mother's parents were killed in a concentration camp and her mother grew up full of grief and anger. Barbara said she has always felt guilty for not making her mother's life better. At one point her mother wanted her to come home and live with her. Barbara said she would have done so, but she wanted her mother to move to a different house because there were too many bad memories in the old family house, and "I knew I would go back to being sixteen." Once her mother was ready to move, Barbara felt guilty because "I didn't make more of an effort to take her into my house." Her overriding guilt, however, is for "not being a good daughter." Her mother used to tell her, "You're a good daughter from a distance."

Barbara added, "I feel my heart was torn out of my body when she died. We had so much unfinished business and I wanted to bring more joy to her. I just wish I had given her a better part of my life, been more there for her."

Perhaps because of this unfinished business, Barbara seems reluctant to let go her guilt. In some cases, guilt can offer a form of security by providing a link with the past and at the same time makes the pain of the loss itself less acute. In fact, some of the daughters who felt guilty admitted that their feelings of guilt were one way to keep their mothers with them. Barbara acknowledged that once she gives up the guilt, she gives up some of the connection, and "I don't feel I have enough to fall back on."

Deborah received many of the same messages from her mother that Willa and Barbara did. When her mother died, Deborah reexperienced the guilt she felt upon leaving her mother more than thirty-five years earlier. She stated that she and her mother were extremely close up until the time she graduated from college and decided to move away. As a child, "I was excessively close, very dependent." She explained that her mother had been frequently ill and she remembered always being afraid her mother would "leave."

It was Deborah, though, who eventually left her mother, now widowed and lonely, and truly dependent on her daughter for companionship, entertainment, and what love was available. "But I had to leave," Deborah said. "I was living at home at twenty-four and my mother was still taking care of me." According to Deborah, that was the first major guilt she was aware of and one that was to diminish in intensity but not to be extinguished, finally, until her own daughter left. "It was then I realized that no mother has a right to expect her children to always be there for her. I was actually pleased to see my daughter off—to help her in any way I could to explore as freely as possible."

Deborah recognizes that, unlike herself, her mother had had few options in life, and, for historical and emotional reasons, had been unable to take advantage of the few that were available. She had been wounded, perhaps, by the world and time in which she grew up—a world in which both brothers went to the university (one graduating from medical school) while she attended business school for six months. "Of course I wasn't angry," she told Deborah. "That's the way it was then."

Once Deborah moved, much of what she now sees as their mutual dependence was replaced by a rather cold and superficial connection. Deborah said that her mother subtly let her know over and over again how sorry and disappointed she was that Deborah left. She once asked her mother what she disliked most about her. "That you left," she answered. Deborah said they kept up the forms: they talked at least once a week, managed several visits a year, and she came to be with Deborah shortly after her twins were born, a time Deborah remembered as a highlight of their times together. "But for the most part, we were conscientious, kind, dutiful, and on some level, very cold." When asked if that was the way her mother would describe their connection, Deborah said "I have to admit, I have no idea what she'd say."

In light of that history, Deborah said, "I'm not surprised, though disappointed, that I couldn't be the ideal daughter at the end. I wanted to be the daughter who would be able to discuss death with her, her fears, her regrets, and tell her I owed everything to her, that she was the world's greatest mom and hold her close." But, she explained, "I couldn't. It was as if I had a spinal injury and hated myself for not being able to run." And then she adds, "after so many years of no intimacy, such intense gestures on my part might have frightened her into an even faster death."

Deborah felt the deprivation of her mother's life and was left with regrets that she couldn't do more. Like Barbara, she has the sense of unfinished business. She said, "I want to do it again. I want to listen more and give less advice. I want to feel compassion, not criticism. I want to fit my rhythm to hers, I want to feel pride in her accomplishments, not disdain for all she gave up. I would have wanted to know the real her. I would have been different. I have this tremendous need to say over and over, 'I'm sorry.' Not because I moved away and made my own life. But because I let her self-protection close me out. I never tried, through sweetness, to tempt her, to bring her into my camp."

Able to achieve a more realistic balance than Willa or Barbara between her mother's unmet needs and her own ability to provide for them, Deborah felt she could eventually come to terms with her feelings. She explained, "My mother and I had no history of her asking and my giving. Even at the end, we couldn't cross our too-familiar lines." What she holds closest is the knowledge that her mother did her best to love a difficult daughter, and, "I did my best to love my difficult mother. Someday I will be at peace with this. I know she is."

NOT GUILTY

While prevalent, guilt is not universal among women who have lost their mothers. Several daughters mentioned they harbored none of these feelings—guilt, regret, or sorrow. "I was clean" was the way Jordana put it. She is one of those daughters who went through periods of rebelliousness, estrangement, and anger, and had carried around a whole witches' brew of negative feelings. Over time, these daughters had worked through those feelings and felt by the end that "everything was on the table."

Another group of daughters who didn't mention guilt had a sense from their mothers that they were a beloved presence in their mother's lives. Three stated that their mothers told them before they died that they had been wonderful daughters; they had nothing to regret. According to Teri, her mother, dying and in a semi-coma, "sat up, looked at me and said 'you did everything you could. I don't want you to cry.'"

The stories of these women suggest that their mothers, no matter what their circumstances had been, were either not depressed or possessed positive natures that overcame their sadness. Not only did they not use their daughters as confidantes to their unhappiness, they did not convey the sense of unhappiness and disappointment that daughters find so easy to discern, even when it is never directly addressed.

When asked if there had been any unfinished business between her and her mother, Helena replied, "Oh, no, we talked about everything while she was dying and even had a conversation checking to make sure we had talked about everything." She asked her mother about the ratio of joy to suffering in her life. Her mother replied that her life had been "80 percent joy, 20 percent suffering. And I asked what was her greatest joy and she said, 'you.'"

Helena and her mother were born in England. Her mother dropped out of school at fourteen and became a hat designer. Helena's father was killed in World War II when she was two. That would appear to be a fair amount of misery. And yet Helena described her mother as "very warm and generous, a very spirited woman." She said that "My mother and I were extremely close. During the time she was widowed, we spent a lot of time together. Even though we were very different, as she came closer to her death I saw more and more ways we were alike. My mother was a dynamic career woman." She talks with great pride of her mother's accomplishments, what a successful buyer she was, a woman who embraced life.

Ella, too, doesn't mention guilt, but only the enormous respect she had for her mother and for what she did with her life. According to Ella, her mother was "a very intelligent woman who could have gone to college." Instead, she raised three daughters and kept the books for her husband's business.

Ella also felt very close to her mother, even though she spent much of her adult life living apart. She said she had a lot of chances to talk with her mother before she died and "I was able to thank her for being such a good 'bubbe' the way her mother had been. She told me 'Your daughter is going to need help—she's losing a good friend.'" The only regret Ella mentioned was for the mistakes she made in her own life, the times she did not listen to her parents.

Those mothers who reassured their daughters, told them they had nothing to be guilty about, did them a great favor. It might be that these daughters had been able to ignore or downplay or not even hear much of what their mothers had to say in terms of advice or criticism, but they were all ears for any positive words their mothers had for them. Mothers, especially mothers of middle-aged daughters, seem to forget that their words, especially their kind ones, still matter. More than they would have ever imagined.

For the rest of us, daughters of dead mothers who ask for another chance to get it right, to be the perfect daughter, here's Jeanne Lohmann's speculation on what would change and what would stay the same.

MOTHER

If you should come up the walk
to the door of my house, if you could
rise in your favorite yellow suit and come
from your grave and find the silver archer
still pinned to the scarf at your throat,
and have your legs work again
so you can walk the miles it would take
to get here to my time of living alone,
what would we find in common?

Over tea and *Scrabble*, the crossword puzzles,
poems you said and I say, aloud in the empty room,
the lists you made and I make to remember
what's essential and to assert that for this day
something waits to be accomplished, we might
give up controversy, be tender and steadfast,
make room for sorting between the layers,
these late leanings without which we die inside,
go to our graves heavy with the weight
of argument and difference. My slower steps
would walk unsteady beside you, my changing eyes
begin to see what I missed.

If you come, will you tell me how to improve my life,
insist I wear a scarf in this cooler weather,
suggest I get a cat for company? Mothering dies hard
as you did, and as I may. What we could do
we did, loved each other. On this November day
of your birth and your death, in my diminished
and reminding house, I clap my hands for delight

in us, go to the door to welcome and let you in,
my sister, my friend [5].

SUMMING UP

Daughters experiencing regret or guilt have found that, for the most part, these feelings pass or greatly decrease in intensity with time. If they remain and incapacitate, however, get in the way of giving and receiving love, and/or interfere with the ability to grieve and move on, it might be worth taking another look at what this guilt really means. It's also important to look for what other feelings guilt might be masking, especially anger, loss, and sadness.

Those daughters who can clearly identify those feelings that are real and those that are false are able to move on with their lives, feel a new form of empowerment, a new opportunity. Once they see their mothers realistically, can distinguish their mothers' pain from their own, separate from their mothers' stories, and acknowledge the compromises they had to make to live their own lives, they will have an easier time letting go of at least some of the guilt. This also requires that they recognize what their mothers, for their part, were and were not able to give them. In this way they can come to terms with the mothering they received or of which, perhaps, they were deprived.

Maybe our generation, we mothers under seventy-five and over fifty, as well as those following us, will be more sensitive to the susceptibility of our daughters. Most women I know tend to be acutely aware of the ramifications of guilt and have tried to make sure that their daughters don't get caught in the same trap. Deborah said that she and her daughter talk about guilt, albeit rather facetiously. "Sometimes when she knows she's disappointed me, she asks, 'Should I feel guilty?' and I do my best to point out she should be looking more closely at what feelings are lurking behind guilt. Those feelings might be the more difficult but ultimately the more meaningful ones."

I would like to leave my daughter free of guilt, at least in terms of her mother. I know that the most powerful amulet against guilt is that we continue to talk openly, and that she clearly distinguishes her life from mine—that she sees that I honor my own life and that I honor her as its touchstone.

If you're among the fortunate daughters who are guilt-free, either because you "feel clean" in terms of your mother's life and death, or because you never thought the words "mother" and "guilt" belonged in the same sentence, think about what you did to make it right and the ways in which your mother helped you to avoid these feelings. Be grateful. Try to pass this affirmation on.

We have to believe that remembering a life with compassion and respect is a far better legacy than guilt, regrets, and remorse. I know that is what I want my daughter to carry in her pocket after I'm dead.

REFERENCES

1. S. de Beauvoir, *A Very Easy Death,* Pantheon Books, New York, 1965.
2. N. C. Kowalski, Anticipating the Death of an Elderly Parent, in *Loss and Anticipatory Grief,* T. A. Rando (ed.), Lexington Books, Lexington, Massachusetts, 1986.
3. A. Rosberger, *When a Parent Dies,* World Book: Health and Medical Annual, Chicago, Illinois, 1996.
4. M. A. Robbins, *Midlife Women and Death of Mother: A Study of Psycho-historical and Spiritual Transformation,* Peter Lang, New York, 1990.
5. J. Lohmann, *Mother* (poem), unpublished, used by permission of the author.

CHAPTER 5

A Mother's Legacy

The play *I Remember Mama,* written by Kathryn Forbes, is a wonderful tribute to a mother. Thinking of our own, however, how many of us could write of mothers who are always wise, helpful, smart? If honest, we're forced to acknowledge that our memories are more apt to consist of images both positive and negative, enabling and constricting, nourishing and debilitating. And this is as it should be. As time passes and we come to accept our loss, work through our grief and guilt, we can begin to view our mothers from a more detached perspective: as women of their time whose lives were formed by their circumstances, personalities, and choices. This is a chance to begin to see them in all their complexity. As real people, not just the one-sided image a child might carry around.

And in seeing our mothers as women in the midst of their lives, in their place in history and not just as our parents, we are free to appreciate their strengths, understand their tragedies, and forgive their shortcomings. Moreover, this perspective opens the door not only for a deeper understanding of our mothers, but also of ourselves as women in our own time.

Most of us who were on good terms with our mothers at the time of their deaths, would like to remember only the best, heeding the admonition, perhaps, never to think unpleasant thoughts of the dead. But by limiting oneself to one dimension of memories, one risks canonizing one's mother. To give due respect to the dead, they should be remembered as real people, not cut-outs. It lends validity to the challenges they faced and how they chose to meet them. It tells us who they were.

People are not simply good or bad. A single character trait may be an asset and a drawback, depending on the context. Sandra, for example, talked about her strong-willed mother in both positive and negative ways. She remembered her mother as a "very powerful and controlling person . . . [who] tried to mold me to her liking." At the same time, she recalled her mother was able to give her "some of her self-discipline and strength" and taught her the idea of "hitching your wagon to a star." Gena, too, recalled her mother as "wistful, and she seemed to feel ashamed because she knew that we knew she could have gone back to finish college, to achieve whatever it was she wanted." And yet, about this same woman, Gena said, "She provided us with tools to think for ourselves."

HISTORICAL CHANGES

Accepting the reality of a mother's life and death, Martha Robbins found, is essential to the final phase in the mourning process. It benefits us as daughters to connect us with ourselves and our mothers' lasting legacy.

> In so doing, the woman is able to accept the historical and cultural influences affecting her mother's life with a deepening sense of respect and compassion. . . . The past relationship with the mother and others is no longer repudiated but reappropriated from a qualitatively different perspective. These daughters, consequently, experience themselves as living their own lives with authenticity [1, p. 217].

To accept the historical and cultural influences affecting a mother's life, you have to first recognize the times in which she lived, and how much has changed between her time and that of yours. It may be easier, then, to see the reasons behind her actions and attitudes.

As stated in the introduction, the women I interviewed for this study were born generally between 1935 and 1945. The majority of their mothers were born before World War I, and represent a generation of women who faced unusual turmoil and often hardship. Many were immigrants who came to this country with nothing, having left their families, perhaps even their languages, behind. Others, born in this country, also suffered great deprivation. An alcoholic father or husband figured in many of the stories. Often impoverished, unemployable, or stuck in dead-end jobs, these women had no choice but to marry anyone who could provide them a home. For them, remaining single was not a choice, nor could love, shared interests, or compatibility be the deciding factor.

So there they were, stuck in loveless marriages, often without even the pretense of fidelity on the part of the husband, with little or no money, and frequently no options or outlets to improve their situation. Adding to the bleakness of their lives was the fact that many of them had lost one or more children in those pre-penicillin days.

The prosperity that began to brighten many lives during the years just after World War I proved short-lived when the Great Depression caused many to lose everything they had so painfully saved. World War II brought yet more hardship with husbands or sons going off for long periods of time and, in many cases, never returning. During the war, many of the immigrants stopped hearing from relatives abroad and so had to assume those family members had died. One could easily add to this list the mothers who lived through the Holocaust, the mothers subjected to the dehumanization of segregation and racial prejudice, and countless other horrors.

It was into these circumstances that many of us daughters were born. Given their own difficult experiences, our mothers' capacity to provide consistent, loving care may understandably have been compromised. Yet even among women who survived such difficult times, there is a significant variation in how they mothered their children, and how their daughters remember them.

Daughters who recognize the obstacles in their mothers' lives seem to have a deeper affection (often, however, accompanied by a feeling of guilt) for their mothers than those who don't. In fact, they found a way to put their mothers into the context of their times so they were able, for the most part, to forgive their mothers their anger, their limitations, their own despair and feel sorrow for them, rather than bitterness.

On the other hand are those daughters whose most profound memories of their mothers are of the unloving ways they felt their mothers treated them. These women did not see their mothers' behavior as a result of their own pain or unexpressed sorrow over the way their lives turned out. As a result, they were not able to feel any compassion, or to have a sense of the reasons behind their mothers' mistreatment of them.

Mostly the complaints had to do with their mothers' relentless criticism, demands for their daughters to be more or better. Ronda summed it up this way: "I spent my whole life trying to please that woman and I never was able to. Now that she is dead, I can finally stop trying." Rachel said even though she felt loved as a small child, she came to realize her mother wasn't so kind or loving. Though trying to take into account the circumstances in which her mother raised her—in Austria, during the war, her husband in the army— Rachel does not excuse her mother's lack of love, and focuses on a pivotal realization when she was twelve or thirteen, sick and in the hospital. "I realized that my mother didn't love me at all. She would come every day and spend as little time as possible and really hated it. I knew that when you are ill, you really start to see through things. I once told her to leave, that I needed some rest and she was so upset. From then on, I realized that she was quite fake, hysterical, and greedy for attention—she was very narcissistic." After her illness, Rachel started feeling more and more estranged.

Five years later Rachel left her home and moved to Texas, but her parents never came to visit, even when her babies were born. She said she knew for sure, then, "there was not much love there. And yet I was a dutiful daughter and went to visit every two years." She thinks her mother's only interest was to show her off. "She couldn't do it often, though, because I was too different so she couldn't show me off to many people."

As mentioned earlier, Robbins questions whether daughters unable to somehow feel the pain of their mothers' lives and deaths, or at least the influences in their mothers' lives that led to harsh criticism and rejection of their daughters, will be able to live authentic lives themselves. She believes that the need to accept one's mother's life in its reality is so important that unless this can happen, daughters will not be able to forgive, and will be sitting on old angers, and thereby making an essential part of themselves unaccessible.

Barbara was another daughter who suffered from her mother's treatment of her; she described her mother as "definitely wounded." Living with memories of her escape from France and the murder of her parents, Barbara's mother used to cry every day. Even when Barbara's aunt would suggest to her mother that "she let it go," Barbara remembered her mother saying, "If I don't cry every day, they [her parents] will be gone forever."

Barbara said that her mother was an actress and there were times when "she was not so heavy." When asked to recall the best parts of her mother, Barbara speaks of her laughter, her musical voice, her intelligence, the way she talked. It was as if her mother were two people: The angry woman and the coquette. It is up to Barbara to integrate the two in order to make her mother's memory whole.

Irene's mother also had a hard life, but instead of showing anger and criticism, she depended on her daughter and encouraged her to succeed. Irene believes one of the most relevant things about her mother is the tragedy of her early life. Her own mother had married early to an alcoholic and had three children. "When my mother was about a year old, her mother was diagnosed with TB and died shortly after." Eventually Irene's mother was put into an orphanage where she stayed until she was eighteen. In the orphanage she contracted TB and polio and didn't walk until she was eleven or twelve. "It was so terrible. Basically," Irene said, "she was illiterate—she could read at about the third grade level and had a lot of trouble with writing. In fact, she was seen as mentally retarded and put into a home for the retarded but didn't stay because they realized she didn't belong there. Of course she felt incredibly inadequate. She was finally released from the orphanage at eighteen and went to live with relatives."

Irene said her mother had no social skills and was ridiculed by the family. She did domestic work and lived a very limited life. The war was a time of opportunity for her. She got a job on an assembly line and, for the first time, she had friends, some money, and a life of her own. Those were some of the best years, her daughter explained. Then she met a soldier and became pregnant. Her family rejected her. She had to take a cab to the hospital to give birth. "They wouldn't let her come into the house—even after I was born. It was very hard. But she encouraged me all along to get ahead. I would be her redemption. I would be her way to get back at the relatives who belittled her. And I succeeded far beyond their dreams."

And while Irene's strongest memories of her mother do not involve anger, she does express sorrow for her mother's lot in life. Even though she was forced to assume the adult role too soon, she appreciates what her mother was able to give her.

It is difficult to understand how adversity can impair one person's ability to genuinely love and nurture a child and allow another to thrive in that relationship. Clearly, there is something that mothers do with and for and to their daughters that can never be reduced to easy observation.

CHANGING TIMES

As if the hardships of early traumatic childhoods, the Great Depression, and two World Wars were not enough to set our mothers' generation apart, there is also the fact that our mothers raised children in a time and place in which men had the choices and enjoyed the opportunities. Deborah was one of several who expressed their frustration with the fact their mothers did so little to take care of themselves, to be a role model for a satisfying, fulfilled life. Daughters like Deborah forgot or did not know what it was like for their mothers in the years before Simone de Beauvoir and Betty Freiden spoke out. Deborah, for example, reported that her father would not let her mother drive a car, preferring to come home from work to drive her wherever she wanted to go. Only when her husband died in 1956 was Deborah's mother finally able to learn to drive. Women, relegated to their "place," were rarely provided goals, stimulation and sometimes, even fun.

Little wonder, then, that our own mothers were not able to take other women, even their daughters, seriously or feel complete as individuals. Several of the women mentioned that their mothers wished their daughters were boys, and many of that generation felt they were nothing without a man. After the death of her second husband, Marcia's mother lived twenty years feeling empty and lonely because she didn't have a man at her side.

Indeed, daughters of my generation are separated from their mothers by a social change of enormous magnitude. Women found their voices and proclaimed that women are equal and should have as many choices. No wonder daughters and mothers had such a hard time communicating with and understanding each other. No wonder so many of the daughters felt their mothers were jealous of them— of their chance to have a career, to speak their mind, even to get a divorce.

Some daughters believed that their mothers' frustrations with their own lives not only led to their being jealous of their daughters (either covertly or explicitly) but also resulted in their being more narrow, more closed down, and consequently less available to the daughters. These mothers tended to deal with their disappointments either by strongly encouraging their daughters to do more or letting their daughters know they could never do enough. They also tended to focus on what their daughters saw as trivial or superficial because of the limitations of their lives. Annie, coming home from a meeting at which she gave the keynote address, reported her mother wanted to know what she wore and was it clean. In some cases, the daughters saw that their worlds were beyond their mothers' imagination, and that their mothers could only address what they were familiar with.

Often the daughters could see their mothers yearning for more, chafing at the restrictions imposed on them by a pre-feminist culture. One of the most moving parts of Simone de Beauvoir's book about her mother's death is the description of her mother's life. She articulates what many of the women I talked with felt about their mothers' lives and the opportunities they missed by living in a more restrictive society. She recalls with sadness how long it took her mother to find the solution to her unhappy life with her husband—to take a job that would give her her own friends and freedom from dependence on her husband. She adds that her mother lived in a time in which people thought that being dependent was natural for a woman, but that it was not all right for her mother. Work, she thinks, would have made it easier to put up with all the parts of her life that were frustrating [2, p. 35].

Gena, too, saw in her mother an unrealized potential and remembered how she admired the accomplishments of others. "I always felt mother had an unfinished agenda, but she would never talk about it." Gena saw her mother as a "very artistic, emotional, sensitive, neurotic person, as someone who might have had a dream but no avenue for realizing it. There was something more she aspired to do. When she met women her age who had accomplished something, she felt bad." Once all her daughters had married and moved away, her mother was left without even the preoccupation of caring for them. Gena thinks her mother died with that feeling, "of not living her dream."

If their lives were filled with despair and frustrated ambitions, mothers tended to treat their daughters either as pet objects who would have better lives and so pushed and praised at every turn, or treated them as extensions of themselves, women who would never "be good enough." Their daughters, in turn, felt either great sadness for their mothers or resentment that their mothers hadn't done more with their lives and anger because they didn't respect their daughters more. If, on the other hand, daughters saw their mothers as enjoying their lives, they tended to be happy with the love and support they received and to view their mothers with respect and to feel the same from their mother.

Many daughters remembered their mothers with awe and admiration, and the importance of their unconditional support. Closely connected to this was the recognition that their mothers' support and belief in them gave them choices they would have not otherwise had. Annie only later came to recognize "how different my life would have been if my mother had not a sense of the possibilities and identified me as the one daughter to realize this." She explains that the only time her mother openly disagreed with her father was when he wanted Annie to leave the academic track and switch to a vocational one, since there was no money. "My mother, who barely spoke English, went to talk to my homeroom teacher who told my mother switching me would be a big mistake." This opportunity, she felt, "was a burden as well as a gift but I have an overpowering sense of feeling so grateful."

Gena, too, believes that despite—or perhaps because of—how unfulfilled her mother was most of her life, she raised her three daughters "to be like men, to get our own profession." She said they all became professionals because their mother was able to transfer what she wanted for herself onto her daughters.

Sometimes, however, this great enthusiasm backfired. If it was too intense, the daughters felt overwhelmed by it. According to Sarah, this unbridled rejoicing in every little accomplishment started to feel manipulating and she hated it. For her, the continual appreciation felt "smothering" and she couldn't wait to escape. She felt her mother's excessive praise was "tyrannical." She believes that, at least in her case, too much praise starts undermining your relationship. "You think maybe your mother doesn't know the situation very well. After a while, I found myself almost beholden to her. I wanted her not to praise all the time." She said that when her mother did criticize her, it hurt. "Maybe more than if there had been less praise."

As noted in the chapter on "Relationships," many of these daughters who felt excessive pressure from their mothers needed to break away at least for a time. For some, it was during adolescence, for others it was from the time they left home at eighteen until they were in their thirties. Most eventually reconciled with their mothers, some with the help of therapy, others on their own, and were able to ultimately appreciate what was positive in the support they did receive.

Faith felt sorry for her mother's life and widowhood—more for the loneliness than for any longing. "Once I moved away, she was truly on her own, a woman not meant to be alone and whose outlook was so narrowed, she just seemed to have too few resources. It was as if she could no longer go after anything." Faith described her mother on those Sundays, "finding little projects and listening to *Madame Butterfly*, and waiting for Sunday to end." Faith recalled that her mother did have a little job for a few years and she had some friends and she took drawing classes and went to movies. But she was alone, and even her children, especially her children, didn't fill any of the gaps. "I'm deeply saddened for her life and whatever circumstances left her to walk through the last twenty years of it alone." Faith said she tried to help, offered suggestions, hoping to get her more involved, but with no success. Faith felt that what her mother hoped for should not have been impossible: a family, and children, and grandchildren to be part of her life. When that didn't happen, she became more and more fearful of anyone getting too close, including, Faith believes, herself. "Finally, she was just proud of the fact that she didn't complain and make a 'nuisance' of herself."

Nora felt her mother, who married when she was only nineteen, had a hard life. She remembered problems with her father who, Nora said, was "very macho, did his male things—hunting and fishing. It was like my father stole her thunder in the relationship. He had a bigger ego and he was musical and he knew everything and she didn't." Nora added that her mother really knew a lot, but the opportunity wasn't there for her to put it into practice. Nora acknowledges that there is a lot about her mother she doesn't know since she moved away so many years before. For example, she said, "I never knew during the years I lived there, my mother used to write children's stories. I was in my late forties when she told me. It was incredible to me. So I used to try to get her to do that again, especially in the later years. She wouldn't. But there was a creativity that was there with her."

Some daughters like Patti seemed to have made a concerted effort to understand their mothers' lives and so to understand their attitudes and reactions to their daughters and how they chose to live their lives. As a result, Patti was very conscious of the differences between her mother and herself.

Patti was struck, not so much by the sadness of her mother's life, but the narrowness of it. She said, "I loved my mother but I didn't really like my mother. She was not someone I would have chosen for a friend. She was very pretentious. When I would tell her about a wonderful experience, her first question was always, what did you wear?" She said her mother made very quick judgments about people and that there "was no depth." As an example, she mentions that her mother insisted on keeping the family home even though she had no money to take care of it or anything else. "What she really wanted was a face lift and for me to loan her $5,000." But Patti insists, "I loved her because she was warm and loving but she was very superficial."

She said that her mother never had any aspirations for her children. Patti's father owned bars, made money, and then lost it because he drank. Still, to her mother, to get married and have children was the most important thing. Patti, who did become a wife and mother, wanted to continue her education after her divorce. Her mother was not pleased with that idea. "I think she resented that I was going back to school—she liked to say 'I think you're getting a little too big for your britches' and she also hated the idea I was studying genetic counseling because she thought it was all about getting women to have abortions and I couldn't change her mind. I had to be very careful not to get beyond her."

When Patti's first marriage ended, she said her mother was there to take her in again. "My mother always needed to be needed. I can remember her saying to me, you come and I'll take care of you. I'll find you a nice man. I always felt she was insecure, even though she was not conscious of it—she would be proud in one way but a little angry in another." Patti said she was the first one to go to college even though her mother didn't encourage it. She had to rely on her school guidance counselors, because there was no help at home. "There was the threat that I was doing something not typical of the family. She watched me raise my kids and was always offended because I pushed them. 'La-di-da. Who do they think they are?'"

Georgia talks about how her father held her mother back. She said her father was a lawyer and her mother had to work in the office because initially he couldn't afford a secretary. "I think she made him the millionaire he became. She was an amazing woman. She was brilliant. She read continually. She could have been anything, and carried a great deal of anger around with her." But, Georgia said, her mother always had an excuse for why she shouldn't do something. She loved to travel but said things like "I can't leave your father alone." And she always had an excuse for not going back to school.

Georgia acknowledged that her mother had no models. Her mother's father was extremely rich until the Depression, when he lost everything and was reduced to peddling wares from a wagon. At that point, her uncle (her mother's brother) went to law school and her mother went out to work. "You obeyed your parents and the boy had a greater likelihood of survival." Georgia found it interesting that her mother, who was always close to her brother, married a lawyer.

Georgia stated that as the years went on her mother became angrier and angrier. There were great mood fluctuations. "You never knew which side of the bed she was going to wake up on. She was stuck in a small southern town and there was no outlet for her brains and she was brilliant. My mother's response to me was that I was too smart for my own good. I do think there was some jealousy. When I left my first husband, I think she was really jealous. She wrote me fearsome letters. I saw a therapist at that time. Part of it was jealousy that I got to leave—I had married a man like my father."

ADMIRATION

By no means were all the daughters' memories bad, sad, or even conflicted. Several daughters focused on the tremendous admiration they had for their mothers. Virginia said of her mother, "Imagine, born and raised on a farm in the Midwest, a little farm girl, she somehow turned herself into a singer and dancer and tried to join every traveling troupe that came through Kansas." Virginia said that even after her mother married, she went off to a dance camp in Colorado and then continued to take classes wherever she lived and even opened her own dance studio. In fact, up until a few years before she died, she was giving dancing and piano classes to children. Virginia marvels at the fact that her mother could conjure up this image and ambition for herself with no role models, no encouragement, just her own guts.

Helena is similarly proud of her mother, whom she describes as a "dynamic career woman and I was so proud of her, so in awe of what she was able to accomplish, how everyone admired her." She explains that her mother rose to her level of professional achievement without any formal education, just her own drive and personality. Helena is also amazed by how many young women adored her. She said that when her mother was dying, the house was full of her young friends who continually dropped by to see her.

Meg's mother, too, is admired by her daughter, not because of her mother's ambition or success in the working world, but because of her presence. She said her mother "had a singular life—she was very generous, everyone was very fond of her. She had such a strong internalized sense of her life, I felt privileged to be part of it." She describes her mother as a true "matriarch"—bright and educated, someone who read voraciously, spoke many languages. There was nothing she couldn't do. I was so grateful to be with her—she was so inspiring."

BRIDGING THE GULF

Given the enormous differences in their lives, it is not surprising that many daughters complain that they never knew their mothers because their mothers "never talked about real things." As Cory said, "when my mother and I started talking about anything that was deep or uncomfortable, my mother would just slide out." And because so many mothers were, at least, perceived as feeling this way, daughters told them very little and felt that their mothers never knew them either. So carefully were the lines drawn, that several women did not even tell their mothers about their divorce until long after the fact. Cory managed to keep that detail from her mother for two years. When she finally did let her mother know, her mother wanted to know what Cory had done wrong.

Simone de Beauvoir said that not only did her mother's limited way of being and feeling make her less fulfilled, but it kept her from knowing herself, which made it impossible for her to know her daughter. She wondered, as did many of the daughters, how her mother could have understood her when she was not willing to look deeply enough to understand herself [2, p. 68].

CHANGING IMAGES

Memories, of course, are not static. They are heavily influenced by the current events of our own lives. When a daughter feels successful, for example, she may be apt to remember her mother's encouragement and faith. When a daughter fails, she is apt to dwell on how critical, how undermining her mother was. As time passes, certain memories recede while others become more important.

Sometimes the focus of memories changes because a daughter discovers something new about her mother. In several cases, daughters reported learning of aspects of their mothers they hadn't known about until after their mothers died. Faith said that she had recently received a bundle of letters her mother had written to a friend when they were both girls. In these letters, her mother wrote about her dreams for the future, of what she hoped to be and do. Faith was stunned to learn that her mother—who hardly ever left the house—had once wanted to go to medical school.

Memories themselves can be unreliable or colored according to our earlier understanding. Recently, I picked up a book that I had read over twenty years before and out fell a letter I had received from my mother while I was reading that book. The letter, in its warmth, humor, and real interest in my life, forced me after all these years to take yet another look at my image of my mother from that time. I was wrong to think she had always been angry. The letter was proof.

As adults, our own experiences often lead to insights into our mothers' lives we couldn't have had as children. Growing older, we discover realities about ourselves that can give us a better understanding of who our mothers were. Cory felt this way. "Now that I am my age, and because I'm alone, I have some appreciation for what my mother must have felt in her life—and what it was like on a daily basis—not to have someone to put their arms around you, or to wish for your children to call and they don't call." Cory was grateful that her mother's death allowed her to see the things her mother did in a "new light." "I feel much closer to my mother and have a stronger appreciation for her life than I did while she was alive and I've wondered why. Why do I feel that now? Why didn't I feel that before she died?"

She answered her own question by explaining, "It might seem far-fetched, but I think while my mother was alive, I kept wanting to do more, be better, be more thoughtful and I felt so guilty because I didn't, even though I had all the time and all the opportunity. When she died, it was too late and somehow the fact that that point had been passed allowed me to be more empathetic, to feel more what her life must have been like. The fear that I could always be doing more kept me in a perpetual state of guilt and when doing things differently or better in terms of her was no longer possible, it was almost as if I was free to acknowledge her completely."

Many daughters said that it is not a matter of changing their impressions; they knew so little about their mothers they hardly had impressions to change. In some cases it seemed obvious to their daughters that their mothers didn't want to share important aspects of themselves; in others, the daughters didn't try to delve beneath the outer self, either because they felt they wouldn't like what they learned or they, like me, were too intimidated by what they perceived to be their mothers' need for privacy.

Even after her death, however, there are things a daughter can do to learn more about her mother. It does seem that the more daughters can come to know their mothers, to understand their motivations and limitations, the more easily they can remember the positive parts of their mothers, the gifts they received from them, and, if necessary, feel compassion for the aspects that hurt or they want to reject.

It takes a little work, but most of the daughters who pursued this avenue found it well worth it. Vivian retrieved her mother's scrapbooks and, looking through them, gained a sense of her mother as a young girl when she was still full of joy and hope. Faith knew that her mother wrote poetry but it wasn't until after her mother died that she sat down to really read it, to get a feel for who her mother was. Deborah went to see her mother's brothers and got them to tell stories of their childhood and to record their memories of her mother as a young girl. Jill spent time with one of her mother's dearest friends and asked her to recall both what she loved and didn't like about her mother.

Paula took a deep breath and focused on what her mother enjoyed and would still:

MOM WOULD HAVE LOVED THAT

Yesterday, baking Mom's favorite
Oatmeal Raisin but instead of raisins,
Cran-raisins.
Mom would have loved that.

The perfect cup of tea.
Steam kissing while tilting the cup.
Cinnamon, orange, cloves and honey

Tingling on tongue.
Mom would have loved that.

Katie in baby bride white
Reverently kneeling for
First Communion.
Mom would have loved that.

JR come back from the dead.
He swaggers again on Friday nights.
Mom would have loved that.

Sneaking a snooze under a mohair throw
Cozy and warm
In broad daylight.
Mom would have loved that.

I smile remembering
How she loved all of that [3].

ETERNAL BOND

Sidney Moss, writing about the persistence of memories and the midlife loss of parents, noticed that some researchers write of "former" parents, suggesting that after a parent's death the bond is gone or diminished. Moss disagrees with this assumption, convinced that the tie persists, not only on an unconscious level, "but viable in the here and now."

> Professionals working with very old people often hear emotion-laden references to parents who died three or four decades ago. In the symbolic remnants of the tie are images of parental supports, protection, or challenge, no matter how constricting or enabling they may have been in the past. The tie is not severed, and the image or presence of the parent continues both in the habitual patterns of daily life which previously involved the parent as well as in subsequent life transitions [4, p. 110].

He points to the basic contradiction—that of separateness and connectedness—that years, even decades, after the parent has died, and, of course, all interactions have stopped, the bond still continues.

It continues in their children's memories, their acceptance or rejection of their legacies.

In thinking back on my mother's life, I am fortunate to come up with a mixed bag of memories. I marvel at the fact that she did everything so carefully and thoroughly. She never did things halfway. I could give her a spot to remove and she wouldn't stop until every last trace of that spot disappeared, no matter how stubborn. She was driven. I used to wonder what she would have done if she could have applied that thoroughness to running a business.

I remember how much more regard she had for men than for women. When I suggested she see a chiropractor, she ignored me. When her brother gave her the same advice, she made an appointment immediately. Her highest ambitions for me were to be pretty and make a good match, while she was proud of my brother's brilliance and encouraged him to do well in school. How I rebelled against all of that, but how could she have thought differently? She had no models herself.

I remember how difficult I made it for her to be my mother. How desperately I wanted her praise and compliments. I still remember with pain and sorrow, begging her as a teenager to tell me I looked pretty and her answering, "What difference does it make what I say, I'm only your mother." How I hated her reticence before I was old enough to recognize that she had no experience in giving compliments and she was frightened of producing a vain daughter.

She used to say, "I want my tombstone to say 'She did the best she could.'" As an imperfect mother myself, I appreciate that sentiment. But I think my mother did much more. She showed me how to laugh, how to accept whatever fate I've made for myself, and ultimately, how to die with grace and confidence. I think it is because I am willing to look again at both the positive and the negative, the similarities and differences between us, that I know what aspects of my mother I have incorporated and what I have made mine alone.

When I find myself trying to set a lovely table, to bring the family together for important occasions, making efforts to keep track of family members by calling, writing, visiting, bringing my Sunday newspaper to my neighbor—I see my mother. When I remove the barrier between myself and others, risk exposing myself for the goal of greater understanding, I know that I am in control of my own destiny. I am not my mother. I am not bound by her constraints.

When I ask for what I want, reject what I don't want, and experience again and again the power of love, I am grateful for the opportunities I have had to be open and free, opportunities my mother never realized.

SUMMING UP

Daughters who are able to remember their mothers in the context of their lives, including the major social and historical events that affected them, are more likely to feel compassion and to see their mothers as multidimensional beings—to praise what was worthy and to accept what was not.

The ultimate good in mourning and accommodating ourselves to loss is to understand and move ahead. If your mother has already died, you can try to re-create her as realistically as you can through stories, anecdotes, her writing, and whatever records she left. Try to grieve a real person, one who lived in her own time.

If you are reading this while your mother is still alive, you would be wise to explore, to try to get to know your mother again. Now that you are both older, she may no longer be as reticent as she was when you and she were younger. And at the same time, you might consider taking off a few of your own protective layers and letting your mother know who you are. You have little to lose at this point. Anything you can learn will help you know yourself better as well. Where possible, try for an authentic relationship, for whatever time is left. Find out, if you can, why she made the choices she did, and how she feels about them in retrospect. When she is no longer with you, you will have a much better chance of remembering a whole person, leaving you free to own those positive aspects and terminate the others.

Either way, the better you can re-create her, the more authentic you will be in your grieving and in your remembering her life.

REFERENCES

1. M. A. Robbins, *Midlife Women and Death of Mother: A Study of Psychohistorical and Spiritual Transformation,* Peter Lang, New York, 1990.
2. S. de Beauvoir, *A Very Easy Death,* Pantheon Books, New York, 1965.
3. P. Karl, *Mom Would Have Loved That* (poem), unpublished, used by permission of the author.
4. M. S. Moss and S. Z. Moss, *The Final Transition,* Baywood, Amityville, New York, 1995.

CHAPTER 6

Taking Care of Ourselves

Talk about ironies. When my mother died, I knew deep in my bones that a lifetime connection had been severed. I had family, friends, work, and yet I felt cold and alone. And the one person I could have shared this with was my mother. She was the one person who would have understood, who might have said, "There, there, it's all going to be all right." It felt like the time I got lost in the bed linen section of Herberger's department store when I was a very small child. I wasn't certain my mother would ever find me. This time no one would page her. There would be no more reunions.

Daughters confront many needs when their mothers die. They may experience a vague, undifferentiated, even primitive sense of longing, like Marian's impulse to call to her dead mother, "You come back here. You can't leave me like that!" In addition, they may be physically, emotionally, and mentally exhausted from tending to their mother and dealing with the details of death.

Many women at this time are at a loss to know what to do or where to turn. They may be long separated from the religion of their upbringing and have no active spiritual practice. Their husbands, children, and other loved ones are eager to have them "back," in their usual roles, and so may have little patience for their grief or need for consolation.

Even friends may not be much good at helping. One of my friends said, "Well, now you're like the rest of us." Another, to whom I was trying to express my feelings that my mother's death would now be part of my life, started to tell me her experiences when her father had died fifteen years earlier. I can't blame them. It is hard to know what to say to people who are mourning. (In fact, I see the local community college offers a day-long course on "How To Express Condolences.")

There are many reasons why friends, family, society as a whole, and even the daughters themselves are confused about their needs and responses. These women are, after all, old enough to be without a mother. The unstated message is that extensive grief for a dead parent isn't entirely appropriate. This attitude encourages grieving adults to deny their feelings, ignore their need for support and the time to work through their grief at their own pace. Moreover, this denial may serve to close off the chance to explore these feelings and possibly transform the grief into something positive and of greater meaning. Added to this is the whole confusion about what adults who lose their parents are supposed to feel, or at least show, after a certain age. I think of Adlai Stevenson who, upon losing to Eisenhower in 1952, said he felt like Lincoln who, when asked how he felt after losing an election, said, "I felt like a little boy who had stubbed his toe in the dark . . . too old to cry, but it hurts too much to laugh."

In the face of this confusion, it is important for daughters to find ways to care for themselves, to discern and address their own needs. The women I spoke with had been successful in finding a variety of ways to help themselves to heal, and to feel more connected to themselves, other loved ones, and the world in general. Some of these ways involved participating in traditional religious rituals, and the planning of funerals and memorials. Some pursued a course of personal exploration or sought psychological insight, whether in the form of support groups or one-on-one therapy. Some found it satisfying to attach to a new "parental figure" while others chose to do something in their own day-to-day existence to connect them to their mothers' memories, like raising the flowers she had loved or preparing their favorite foods. Visiting a site that was meaningful to both the mother and daughter was another way daughters found comfort.

RITUALS

In traditional religious practices, a death is accompanied by a series of rituals designed to honor the deceased and comfort the bereaved. Those daughters who participated in such traditional observances spoke of the strength and healing they derived from them, whether or not they were actively practicing that religion at the time.

Cory found the Roman Catholic rituals comforting both as she helped prepare for her mother's funeral and during the service. She said that right after her mother died, there were so many decisions to be made—how many days she would be laid out, the selection of the casket and so on, and at the same time she kept wondering why they were doing those things. Even though she was struck by the "absurdity of the whole process," she realized, "There is something about the rituals you do. It makes you put one foot in front of the other, like greeting people at the funeral home, which we did for two days. It was very hard to do. Then we had the funeral; we all participated in the process. My nieces and nephews participated and they sang—all of them were very involved in the mass and choosing the songs. They all have amazingly beautiful voices and that had meaning for me." Cory said she couldn't help noticing how all the grandchildren and great-grandchildren represented a living legacy of her mother's, and that they were only there because of her.

Koru, who follows Buddhist traditions, described the events following her mother's death. "There was no struggle. She just coughed one evening and stopped breathing. I knew not to call 911 but I did call the doctor who said 'let her go' and it was so gentle. But I knew it didn't end. I knew she could still hear me. I just played chanting tapes for three hours with her. That night the Buddhist priest came and chanted at her bedside. It was as if the roof and sky opened up and all boundaries disappeared. The room was energized, just filled with another energy. I suspect that helped. My sister and I could tell when my mother's soul left her body—there was such serenity in the room—as real as if you saw it with your own eyes. Not the end of anything." During the prescribed forty-nine days of grieving that followed, Koru read the traditional prayers out loud, saying good-bye.

Rita took great comfort in the orthodox Jewish rituals of mourning. "I credit traditional Jewish mourning rituals, which propel mourners head-on through their grief, with buttressing me during this difficult time. Although I do have my moments and will for a long time, I really feel that having gone through this has helped me a great deal."

She explains that an essential part of the process is Shiva—the seven-day period immediately following burial when mourners stay at home and community members bring prayers and condolences. "It meant a lot that friends cared enough to interrupt their daily life to show they cared." Traditionally, during Shiva, mourners are released from economic and social obligations, and encouraged to accept the all-encompassing nature of their grief. "We cover mirrors, tear a part of our clothes, avoid parties—in many ways deprive ourselves of those little mechanisms for cheering ourselves up because we're supposed to be in mourning."

Rita felt particularly supported by the communal embrace that enveloped her in her most intense grief. "I didn't have to go to a grief counselor because all [my feelings] came out . . . There's no better place than among the people who've known you best all these years."

Those who have moved away from formalized mourning rituals found that assuming the tasks of planning the funeral or memorial services was very healing. Many daughters spoke of the importance of creating a personal tribute to their mothers' memories. Madeline, for example, was able to replace some of her sense of loss and abandonment with the personal pride she took in making all the funeral arrangements, including shipment of the body. "I took great comfort in planning my mother's memorial service. It was, in a way, my last gift to her and one that I took great pleasure in. I invited her friends and those of my friends who had made a connection with her. I prepared or bought all of her favorite foods and I read things she had written and something I wrote for and about her. People in the group recounted their memories and I had a chance to greet all of her friends, most of whom I would not see again, as a special envoy from her."

Linda, too, spoke with great pride of her mother's memorial service, for which she played a big part in planning. "It was beautiful." She, her sisters, and their father worked together to make the arrangements, picking the place and time, getting the flowers, arranging who would speak, deciding on the music. She remembers how beautiful the chapel was. "About 200 or 300 people came—an enormous outpouring of love and caring. It was so helpful for me to see how loved and admired my mother was. Everyone was so proud of my mother. It was a great tribute from the whole family. We were very satisfied that we had done justice to her memory. We put a lot of effort into everything. She would have loved the party." And she added, "It was very healing."

Several other daughters incorporated rituals from different religions to create a personal tribute, to connect with the past and present, to feel loved, or to share in the passing. Annie said what she found most important was deciding, after the funeral, to go back to her house and call a few people to come over. "They all came and there was a wonderful comfort being with those I cared for and who cared for me."

PHYSICAL COMFORTS

Especially in those cases where the daughter has been involved in the care of her dying mother, anything that comforts the heart or the body seems to have great healing potential. Vivian says the massage she had during the two days between her mother's death and the funeral was one of the most precious things she could have done for herself. She says she needed to be touched deeply and in a way "that asked nothing of me. It enabled me to let go of some of my protectiveness and really feel those deep, unprotected places. Afterwards I felt much stronger, more prepared for what was to come."

Sarah found similar release during a Shen workshop she attended a week after her mother's death. (Shen is a physio-emotional release therapy during which there is a balancing of energy.) The experience enabled her to cut through the layers she had built up during her mother's decline, and she was able to cry from a very deep place—for all the guilt, all the loss and regret. "It was a truly visceral experience. All the parts of the body which contract because of grief and pain are opened up in a gentle, non-invasive way."

Food, too, can be another form of self-care. This is how Carolyn Miller comforted herself when she received the news about her mother:

FOOD

When they told me my mother had taken a turn
for the worse, I called up the airline
and made a reservation to go home. Then
I went into my kitchen and made hot cocoa,
just like we made back in the old kitchen
in Missouri: first a paste of Hershey's cocoa
and sugar with a little milk, then more milk
until it was the right color of cocoa brown.
I drank it all at once, and I could feel
the hot, sweet liquid burning down my throat,
and I knew I was alive. I went to the store
and bought strawberries, lots of them, three boxes

of shining, taut new California strawberries
almost as big as plums, and I bought bread and asparagus
and new red potatoes, tiny ones like the kind
my father used to grow, and I went home and made
creamed asparagus and new potatoes, and strawberries
sprinkled with sugar so that a sticky red juice collected
in the bottom of the bowl. I ate and ate,
because I was alive, and because I had
an appetite, like my mother had when she loved food
and when she was too heavy, before
she began to waste away to nothing and couldn't eat
at all. I ate the creamed vegetables and too much bread,
and I thought about all the years my mother had cooked
for us, so much food, the creamed chicken with biscuits,
the potato salad, the pies, the tall cakes—honest, unadorned
dishes from the Betty Crocker cookbook and the red-and-white
Good Housekeeping book and the mysterious old
falling-apart green book with the yellow-brown pages.
And I thought about how my mother's food
had made me feel that I was safe and loved and cared for,
and I kept on eating bread and vegetables, and then
I ate the strawberries, so many that for once
I had almost all the strawberries I wanted, red and
streaming in the bowl, sliced open to reveal
their shimmering flesh and their knot-shaped hearts [1].

SUPPORT

Other women found comfort in being with women who were
making the same transition. In fact, Robbins writes that the story of
each woman she talked to illustrated the crucial importance of a
support network in the process of mourning, of being with those who
can recognize and accept one's need to work through the many layers
of grief triggered by the loss of one's mother. She goes on to say that if
mourning is to truly lead to a "transformation," women need more
than just support, consolation, and comfort. Interactions with others
must also extend the possibility for formulating new images of their
mothers, and themselves in relation to their mothers, so old images
can be reconfigured in more honest ways [2, p. 238].

Support can come from family, friends, support groups, and even
professionals. One might expect that those closest would offer the
greatest understanding. Yet many that turn to their family for this
comfort or support often discover that their expectations and needs

conflict with those of other family members. Kennedy found that if you are seeking stability and continuity at the time of bereavement, you probably will be disappointed to find that your family is also changing [3, p. 107]. They, too, are coming to terms with loss and change in their own way and often you can't even count on your nearest and dearest. Those connected to you most closely, your mate or significant other, are apt to start feeling lonely and may want you back the way you were. Linda said that her partner was very tender and patient for about five days after her mother died. He would hold her while she cried and listen attentively while she talked about her loss. But then the time was up. Long before she was ready, "He was finished. He had decided that enough time had gone by and I should shape up." This was the attitude of other women's close connections as well. This is not to say the significant others were necessarily lacking in sensitivity, but for their own reasons, they were unable to accept that the mourning process moves at its own pace, that each person reacts to grief in her own way.

It was clear that the women I talked with found for themselves through trial and error what did and didn't provide what they needed. Many turned first to friends, hoping they would provide the comfort they were searching for. The results were mixed. While some friends do provide a support system, others, missing "the old you," the one who was eager to hike, share a coffee, laugh at a good story, may decide for themselves what is good for you. They will tell you that you have spent enough time feeling sad; it's time you get out and do something. Other friends, you may find, simply withdraw. Your pain might feel too close to their own—or to what they anticipate feeling in similar circumstances.

Sue found that "You have to be willing to speak up for yourself, to tell your friends what will make you feel better, what you want and don't want from them. You may have to explain that you appreciate their concern, but you are working at your own pace." She adds that you have to "be willing to tell them that what you want is to just have them listen, maybe you'll appreciate their advice at a later date." Several daughters reported that it was helpful to tell those closest to them when they wanted a hug or just to be held. And, of course, to let them know when what they really wanted was to be left alone.

Like many, I found my child to be a source of reassurance and comfort. Not everyone who has a child feels that way and not everyone whose mother dies has children. But for me, my daughter was the person who could best identify with my feeling of loss, since it was only a short leap for her to imagine her own mother dying. And because she felt a deep love for her grandmother, it was her loss, too. She knew what I was going through because she shared some of the same feelings.

Women I talked to mentioned what "bricks" their kids were. Jordana had always been grateful for the fact her boys loved their grandmother so much. It not only pleased her mother, but allowed Jordana to feel a little less guilty for the love she had withheld from her mother. She said that her older son helped her make the life and death decision about her mother's medical care, and gave her important advice at the same time. He told her, "I know you can't stand the suffering—but you have to make that decision for her [Jordana's mother]. If you're not clear, you'll be sorry for ever." They gave Jordana a valuable perspective, too. As the boys were talking about what Jordana would want when her time came, one told her, "If I know you, you'll be giving orders at the last minute." It was a chance for her to explain she will want them to make the decisions she can't. In this situation, as well as many others, the death of a mother propels her daughter to start thinking about her own.

SUPPORT GROUPS AND COUNSELING

Especially in the absence of strong support from friends, partners, and children—or even in addition to these—many women found joining a support group very comforting. Some sought out groups within a month after their mothers died; others waited as long as a year when it appeared they were not going to shake off their depression by themselves.

Jorie is one of those who found joining a bereavement group very helpful. She said that her husband and her grown kids were eager for her to "stop moping" and they too soon ceased to be a source of comfort. She read about a group called "Motherless Daughters" and signed up. She said that the support she received from sharing her feelings and experiences was invaluable. Group members had many issues in common—even seemingly insignificant ones. Jorie was amazed that when she tearfully admitted to the group that she didn't know what she was going to do with some of her mother's prized possessions that she, herself, hated, almost everyone admitted having the same problem. The group came up with a lot of helpful suggestions for each other. Faith, too, found a focused support group extremely helpful and feels the wisdom of the group leader helped all the women grow in important ways.

Don't be afraid to try counseling if you feel it would be helpful. It may be useful to work with a professional to examine the meaning of the death and your grief, especially if you feel you are having unusual difficulty during this time. Counseling can also be an opportunity to gain assistance in exploring larger issues that may take on particular relevance at this time, such as reconciling with the past or your mother's memory, or discovering what changes might be possible for you to make that would enrich your life.

Meg reports that the therapy in which she participated about six months after her mother died really "helped me put the pieces together." She said that she finally decided to seek help because she had become "paralyzed with indecision." She felt great anger at her brother (with whom she had never been close) and found it impossible to forgive him for having given her no help when she was dealing with her mother's very troubled final months. She was trying to figure out what kind of a relationship, if any, she wanted with him. In addition, the guilt and grief she felt over failing to protect her mother from so much suffering plagued her every move. She said that within relatively few sessions, she was able to decide that it was okay to let her mother go. By working through areas of guilt throughout her life, she began to see, "I did a good job caring for my mother, even though I couldn't take care of her the way she had cared for me when I was young." Mostly, though, she adds, "I am extremely grateful for having the opportunity to see my choices. That was one of the most important gifts I received from the therapist."

PERSONAL EXPLORATION

Many professionals advocate healing through self-exploration. Dreams and journals are two approaches women found helpful.

After a parent has died, there can be a comforting sense of continuity in dreaming about the parent while one is struggling to come to terms with the loss. Most therapists feel that dreams have the power to help make conscious whatever is being repressed or minimized. Vivian, for example, recognized that at the same time her dreams were of troubling images, so much so that she awoke fearful and depressed, she went through her days as if nothing was wrong. She knew this dissonance suggested she was not in touch with her own feelings and that it was worth looking into with a therapist. Others, in similar situations, found dream groups very helpful.

Not everyone is proficient at "conscious dreaming" but even those who downplay the importance of dreams, find it worthwhile to make the extra effort to try to remember and record their dreams at times of great change and/or loss. This is something that you can experiment with.

Over time, dreams can help you learn about yourself and the nature of what you are going through. After her mother's death, Sue kept a dream journal. At first, she found that all of her dreams had to do with a car crash, even though her mother had not died in an accident. In fact, Sue, herself, had always been terrified of automobile accidents. Through her recordings she saw that with each dream she got a little closer to the disaster before she woke up. Finally she dreamt of the accident itself. She was in the car with her mother when the car went over a cliff. They landed on soft sand and she and her mother got up and walked away. She realized that with this dream, she had acknowledged some sort of safe landing—for herself and her mother. She felt she had turned a corner in her grief and was ready to move back into the world.

A journal can serve as an invaluable resource during grief, not only for recording dreams but also for exploring the many faces of grief. As the jumbled thoughts and feelings come to the surface, they can be written down in an unedited stream of consciousness. Many daughters kept a daily record of all they were experiencing and reported a sense of relief in expressing their thoughts in words, as though a burden had been lifted. Lynne found putting on paper all the conflicting and overwhelming feelings and experiences was very cleansing and comforting. She realized that by reflecting on what she had just written, she could recognize some sort of order beginning to take shape in the midst of the chaos.

PERSONAL NEEDS

As time goes on, it is important to stay in touch with what you need—from others, from yourself, from your surroundings. Many daughters improvised small changes in their lives after discovering the death had affected them in unexpected ways.

Some daughters, especially those who saw their mothers often or were in the habit of caring for them, felt particularly at loose ends after their deaths. Finding a "mother replacement" seemed to be one way to work through the loss.

Karen had always liked Beth, a woman her mother had been friendly with, although Karen would never have developed a separate relationship with her while her mother was alive. She felt that might even have provoked some jealousy in her mother, and Karen felt she had room for only "one old woman" at a time. Beth shared Karen's pleasure in music and poetry, and Karen found her warm and open. Beth had no children of her own and had always liked Karen, as well. Once Karen could accept that she was not being disloyal to the memory of her mother, they developed a fine friendship. Karen, by now in the habit of doing little things for her mother, was happy to do them for Beth, including inviting Beth to family gatherings.

Barbara made an effort to grow closer to her mother's sister who lived in Europe and whom she barely knew. When her aunt told her, "You are OK, in fact you are better than OK," Barbara said she felt as if she had found a safety net. It was especially helpful because her mother had been excessively harsh and critical of Barbara.

Sometimes it's not even the "replacement" companion, but the continuity of doing for another that provides solace. Shortly after my mother died, a close friend had a stroke and was left partially paralyzed. Before my mother's death, I would have called every few weeks to say hello. Afterwards, however, I had honed my instincts for doing extra shopping, bringing a little gift, sharing a Saturday lunch; so once I had that space and habit in my life, I was happy to continue doing the little things for my friend that I had done for my mother.

Other activities had meaning as well. Several women mentioned how much comfort they got from going to visit their mothers' graves. Madeline described her ten-hour journey to the cemetery and said, "I could feel this presence—grieving being lifted in the cool wind across the desert." She explains, "I needed to visit her grave, to look at her headstone. I find it important to be in a place where others grieve the dead. I talk to her about what she's missing, what her grandchildren are doing, what I've been doing."

Joanne buried her mother on the side of a mountain. "I go to sit near her. In fact, I feel I cannot leave Utah now. She will be all alone." Jasmine lives close to where her mother is buried and says she goes there when she is upset. "I just sit and cry and brush off her tombstone." She says the site has particular significance to her because her mother selected it three years before she died.

Time, also, can become an important gift to oneself. I bought myself time when I kept my mother's apartment an extra month. I could go there at my leisure, sort through her belongings, and select out the things that mattered. My brother and I decided what we would give away, what we would save for the grandchildren and great grandchildren, and what I would take home for temporary storage because we didn't know what else to do.

The next step was to begin on the items I had stored in my basement. I gave myself an arbitrary timetable of a year to sort, sift, and decide. At first, everything I touched evoked tears and memories. The purse she had carried the last time I saw her for lunch. Her eyeglasses, her handkerchiefs still redolent with her perfume. As the year wore on and the pile diminished, I was still connected, but the items became more "just things." By the end of the year, I felt very differently and could comfortably make decisions. Had I had to go in and dispose of everything immediately, I would have been overwhelmed with grief and loss.

Terri had a similar experience. On the day of the funeral, she said to herself, "I'm not dealing with anything now," and went away for four months. When she returned, she had a garage sale for those items she "couldn't stand," and put her mother's house up for sale. It sold the next day to a family she liked. Terri rented a truck, filled it up with the things she wanted and returned home.

ADDITIONAL GIFTS

There were two more gifts that daughters mentioned they were able to give themselves in the wake of their mothers' deaths, more abstract than the others but ultimately more significant. The first is providing for yourself where your mother left off: giving yourself the direction and encouragement and even the nurturing you might have still hoped for from your mother, whether or not you ever actually received it. Kennedy reminds us that even though we may not look to our parents for active parenting once we become adults, we may nevertheless have fallen into the habit of expecting that "someone else" will make things better, protect us, or give us what we will not give ourselves [3, p. 110].

"To my surprise," Elaine said, "within six months after my mother died, I started giving myself credit for each and all accomplishments. Not only that, I finally started doing my own hems, something my mother, even into her eighties, had done for me." Barbara has found something similar, "I really think I'm emerging into a better person. I am more self-validating of who I am." She said she was looking forward to the time that she would feel the sense of liberation that she knew could be part of her life, once she's willing to change her connection to her mother.

These changes, in turn, can lead to the best gift of all, the ability to internalize and identify with those aspects of our mothers we most valued. Linda said that when she saw at the memorial service how loved her mother had been, she wanted to find those parts of herself that were like her mother. In the same way, Natalie, recognizing all the honors her mother had received for her community involvement, decided then that she would make a real effort to give back, in the way her mother had. It is by internalizing the dead, too, that we complete the process of mourning.

SUMMING UP

If someone had said to me before my mother died, "You're going to feel lost for a while, your universe is going to feel as if something was taken from it. You might even feel, for a bit, like someone just knocked the wind out of you," I wouldn't have believed that person. If this same person had suggested I think about how I would then take care of myself, make sense of the loss, incorporate, and even learn and grow from it, I would have had no idea what she was talking about. A mother is old, she dies, life goes on, I would have thought. I had a lot to learn. And I'm still trying to benefit from what I learned from her death—about her, about me, and about life.

It seems essential that most daughters, no matter what their age when their mothers die, find the time and means to take care of themselves. It is a time to be selfish, to think about what you need, what will make you feel better while you process this change in your life. If the first thing you try doesn't make you feel better, try something else. But keep trying because until you are centered and whole, you will not be able to move on.

Our culture does little to prepare us for the finality of death—we are taught to acquire and replace, not to lose or let go. Death is seen as a defeat, not as a natural part of the life cycle. Consequently we have trouble even accepting its reality and try to pretend it's just been a bad dream. In fact, for weeks after a death we might catch a glimpse of some small, white-haired woman or hear a familiar voice and think for just a second, there she is! She is still alive. But as the months and years pass, the finality burrows in, and we accept that our loss is permanent and final.

Sooner or later, all daughters must find for themselves what will make them whole again—rituals, planning of funerals and memorials, friendship and family, a chance to sit with others in the same situations, graveside visits, dreams, journals, meditations, the time to say good-bye, the time to let one season pass into the next.

In this poem, I was thinking about making my mother's cake for the first time since she died. In writing it, I discovered a kind of finality and even joy:

FOOD FOR THE DEAD AND THE LIVING

Sun finally shines.
But my mother is too dead
to enjoy it.
I bake her favorite cake,

A cliche, angel food—
the way you break the eggs,
separate the nucleus of life
from what protects it,
ignore the sun-ball yolks,
focus on isolating cloudy albumen

Then whip those whites
full of sweet smells of orange, almond,
Pacific breeze, wait
for the mystery—how each time
they thicken, turn silky, then white,
rise into peaks

The very act of *gently folding*
flour, sugar into the whites,
giving air no chance to escape,
sliding batter into the pan,
into the oven
where it continues its rise—
an act of faith.

The cake, too light to be held aloft
by only egg whites and flour,
sits like an offering.
I think she's applauding.
Maybe even welcoming
this day of sun.
As if it is all beginning [4].

REFERENCES

1. C. Miller, *Food* (poem), unpublished, used by permission of the author.
2. M. A. Robbins, *Midlife Women and Death of Mother: A Study of Psycho-historical and Spiritual Transformation,* Peter Lang, New York, 1990.
3. A. Kennedy, *Losing a Parent, Passage to a New Way of Living,* Harper, San Francisco/New York, 1991.
4. D. Lutovich, Food for the Dead and the Living, in *The Green Hills Literary Lantern,* North Central Missouri Writers Guild, 1995.

CHAPTER 7

Holding On and Moving Forward

With the death of their mothers, daughters often feel pulled in two opposite directions by the need to preserve the past and the desire to look ahead to the future. By this stage of their lives, most women have become quite good at the balancing act between keeping and letting go. They started learning this lesson with their children, perhaps husbands and lovers, even jobs and homes. The period surrounding her mother's death is an especially important time for a daughter to be able to find a satisfying balance as she finds ways to value the past even while moving into the next life stage.

Many daughters use this time of transition between their mothers' deaths and total reentry into the world to start thinking (even if not consciously) about which aspects of their mothers they will include in their lives and how they can use their mothers' deaths as spurs for their own personal growth. It's a time of many demands and concerns, both tangible and intangible, beginning with the disposition of their mothers' possessions, incorporating memories, rethinking connection to family, taking another look at goals, examining what is and is not owed to others, as well as integrating their experience and creating a new relationship with their mothers.

THE POWER OF "THINGS"

Among the first major decisions the daughter must make is what to do with her mother's belongings. It is difficult not to feel that this disposition is symbolic and even sets the stage for future decisions. Simone de Beauvoir, writing about items left in her mother's apartment after her mother's death observed that, "Everyone knows the power of things: life is solidified in them, more immediately present than in any one of its instants" [1, p. 98]. No wonder the task seems so formidable and cannot be taken lightly.

Like many, I faced the task of sorting through and disposing of my mother's possessions once the items specifically earmarked for her daughter, daughter-in-law, and granddaughters had been distributed. While I knew that what remained were "just things," they were the objects she had owned, fretted over, cared about and thereby invested with meaning, even love. A part of her was in them.

First of all, I had to deal with some small discomfort for wanting to give almost all of her furniture away. Some of the pieces dated back to long before our family home was sold, shortly after my father died in 1955. I could still see myself sitting on the grey couch with my first date more than forty years ago (it had always been uncomfortable). Nostalgia aside, neither my brother nor I had any use for it. Without too much trouble, I convinced myself that the dead don't care about possessions and there are many living who do. We gave almost everything to an agency that helps resettle refugees. They seemed delighted to have all of it and even sent a truck to the back door of the building. (Obviously, they often cart away furniture from apartments of deceased residents and so exercised discretion.)

I gave my mother's good dresses, scarves, and record albums to Betty, a woman she had become friendly with, who told me that my mother had promised her the scarves. This was a revelation. I had thought my mother, like me, had been oblivious to the fact she was dying. Instead, my mother had discussed her death with Betty some time before her final hospital stay. Knowing this, I figured she would want Betty to have the other things as well. Among the items were some lovely dresses that we had gone shopping for only two months earlier. Years before, whenever my mother would consider buying a rather expensive piece of clothing, she would jokingly ask me if I would promise to wear it if she died before it was worn out. Since I had not made a firm commitment to these particular dresses, I felt I was off the hook.

Other items were not so easily discarded, and these I had to take home. I couldn't part with the coats that were so much a part of her. Nor the red blazer she had loved; I have a picture of her wearing it—she looks so pleased with herself. I kept and wear the watch and earrings my father gave her just before he died, and placed my mother's prized hurricane lamp in the middle of my living room, even though it doesn't go with anything else I have. I also needed to keep her purses and anything she had made.

The enormous portraits of my brother and me as children along with a few other things I could neither keep nor give away, I boxed up and labeled for my daughter to deal with when I die. I think she'll be able to dispose of them without too much trouble.

Within six months, I came to terms with the coats and blazer. I knew an elderly, poor, and very dear woman who is the same size as my mother. I asked her if she would do me the favor of taking my mother's coats. She said she would be delighted and asked if I would feel bad if I saw her wearing them. I assured her that it would make me—and my mother—very happy. The red blazer I sent to my niece. In one way or another, I got rid of the items I didn't need, kept what made me feel close to my mother, and stored those I could neither keep nor give away. So she lives on, in dozens of ways, and, at least indirectly, provides some comfort.

Terri also felt good about the way she integrated her mother's furniture into her house, and how well her mother's pieces complemented each other. Terri was one of several daughters who felt that the way she incorporated her mother's belongings into her life symbolized other kinds of accommodations as well.

After her mother died, Jasmine turned her guest bedroom into "my mother's room" with all of her mother's belongings. "My mother saved cartons of sewing stuff. I can't get rid of it, I can't throw her things out." Much to her surprise, Jasmine ended up keeping her mother's dog as well. She thought she'd give it away because she had always been allergic to dogs. After she had it home for a while, she found she could stay with it longer and longer without getting sick. "Laddie," she felt, "is my mother's child, her last thing."

While some daughters struggled over how to dispose of unwanted items left by their mothers, other daughters were terribly disappointed not to receive any token or remembrance of their mothers'. Marcia couldn't believe that her mother had not earmarked a single item for her first-born daughter in her will. So, ahead of the appraiser, she took a few special things that reminded her of her mother, including her mother's baby pillow and the love letters her father had sent to her mother more than fifty years before.

Cory was thrilled when her sisters decided she should have their mother's ring. "All the time I was growing up, I would look at this ring and I would think it was the strangest ring and why did she have such a funny ring? When my sisters gave it to me, for some reason, it was very beautiful."

KEEPING THE CONNECTION

Beyond tangible keepsakes and tokens, daughters reported many ways by which they maintained a close connection to their mothers. Some purposefully incorporated their mothers' memories into their daily lives through activities, gestures, and habits, while others mentioned encountering their mothers through dreams and other phenomena, such as psychic appearances, which seemed to happen unbidden.

Patti felt it important to keep her mother's memory alive "by talking about her a lot" with her family. "My girls and I imitate her— her many comments and expressions, what we call 'granny-isms.' Last weekend was Easter and mother always did a big thing for Easter. I hadn't done one for years, but I did it to keep her present, try to remember her."

Robbins could have been writing about Patti when she wrote about the importance of both identifying with and taking on those parts of the mother her daughter most valued. In this way, she explains, the daughter is able to truly accept her mother's death, and at the same time, remain connected by bringing her to life inside herself " [2, p. 165].

Patti stated, "Sometimes I ask myself what would I want from my family when I die. Well, keep me from being gone. Remember me. Value the things I cared about. I know I would want my kids to do things my way after I go. Ask, 'How would Mom do that?' It honors the person. My brother can actually imitate her voice and we laugh. And my mother would love it."

Beverly noticed, "Before my mother died, I'd say oh no—I'm just like my mother. Now that she's dead, that's changed—it is not such a bad thing to consider." After her mother died, she put a photo on the kitchen counter to talk to. At one point, "I got mad when I realized some of her old rules from the fifties were still influencing me. I didn't want that and put the picture away but then I came to grips with the past and treasured her picture." It provided a presence she found comforting and she felt that the kitchen was the right place. "It's where we would sit and talk."

Photos, flowers, conversations—even a bargain—all became ways of keeping a special connection to the deceased. Helena, who came to respect her mother's interest in "things," said that her mother had always loved to shop. At one time, Helena explained, she thought her mother was a superficial collector, but by the end of her mother's life, Helena realized how much substance her mother had. On her mother's birthday, she lit a candle, went to Macy's, and found a bargain in her memory. "As I put my purchase in the bag, I said to her, here's looking at you, Mom."

Vivian's mother used to love to put up preserves, especially to make jam. She was a Midwesterner where that was a way of life. After she died, Vivian and her daughter started their tradition of picking berries, making jam, and then bringing the jars to as many of her mother's friends as they could.

Many daughters maintained their sense of closeness by talking to their mothers or by visiting the grave site. Joanne had a particularly hard time after her mother died; she felt homeless, disappointed by her friends and in-laws whom she hoped might help to fill in the emotional gaps left by her mother's death. "Whenever I need to talk to my mother, I go to sit near her grave. I feel I cannot leave the area, leave her alone." Sukie felt she lost a good listener, a good friend, but said, "I feel a line—between when she was alive and now—but her presence is with memories, feelings, and pictures—sometimes I feel like I'm talking to her." Emma also talked to her mother frequently but wondered sometimes if her mother didn't say, "Here she is, bothering me again."

Not a sentimentalist, Georgia feels closest to her mother in the garden and uses flowers to honor her mother's memory. "I don't go back to the grave. I don't believe she's in there. I talk to her some days. I think she's in the things she did and in the garden, in the enormous camellias."

Writing is another way that daughters can choose to keep and let go of their mothers. Poets and non-poets alike find writing about them helps to keep their mothers alive and acknowledge their deaths. In her poem, Jeanne Lohmann, writing just before the first Mother's Day after her mother died, speculates about her mother's life.

In heaven, my mother

will be "at home" in her country house
and invite authors for tea
when she reads they will listen
amazed she's learned so much

by heart   when they read she will listen
and nod *Amen*   the exalted conversations will flow

she will offer refreshments: sandwiches
and fruit, gingerbread   there will be candles
and fine linen napkins edged with lace,
silver vases for violets, lilies of the valley
like the ones in her wedding bouquet
when she climbed out the bedroom window
while Grandpa was at the church supper,
eloped with my father to Greenville

she will show visitors her garden of larkspur
and bearded iris, scarlet hollyhocks,
peonies, yellow roses like "sunshine
spread as thick as butter on country bread"
(she will read Riley, yes, sure that heaven
is the midwest—Ohio, maybe, Indiana)

in the grand library of arcane books and esoteric
traditions she will sit up late
writing stories and essays   (they will be published)
her dictionary will answer the most difficult crosswords
her vocabulary surprise the angels

guests will stay as long as she wants
my father will sing and tell stories
they will not worry   they will be happy

everything she remembers
will be perfect   if she has a body
all the parts will work

if there is time
she will tell
by blowing seeds
off the dandelion

as many breaths as it takes.

                                    J. Lohmann

UNCONSCIOUS CONNECTIONS

Dreams often provide an opportunity for daughters to once again "touch" their mothers—and vice versa. A year to the week of her death, my mother showed up in three dreams on three successive nights. The first two dreams were rather contentious and had to do with unfinished business from my childhood. All the issues were ancient, ones I had been unable to come to terms with and could not discuss with my mother. So although I am not one who has studied or knowingly practices "conscious dreaming," after the second dream (in which I could actually hear the whine in my voice), I told myself that I was too old to be fighting these old fights; either have a reconciliation dream, or don't dream at all. On the third night I dreamt my mother and I were in Paris. She was ecstatic, so happy to be there, in fact, happier than I had ever seen her. I asked her if she wanted to rest before going out for dinner while I went to the D'Orsay. Resting had always been very important to her. She said absolutely not. She had no intention of missing anything. I was the one who brought her there. I was the one who gave her such pleasure. Resting could wait. It was a very healing dream.

Annie also had a dream that surprised her. "I was involved in a new relationship with a man who literally had no money. In the dream, I said to my mother, 'I've met someone, he's very nice, and I think you would like him.' She smiled, and then I told her that he had no money, and she smiled again as if to say it doesn't matter. That surprised me, because money was always an issue."

Liz and her two sisters had talked to their mother by phone all the time, sometimes as many as two or three calls a day. Liz said that after her mother died, she dreamt that her mother was trying to call her on the phone, that she had something important to tell her. Each sister had the same dream.

What struck me about my own dreams and some of those reported by others was the fact that the mother in the dream was different from the way she had appeared in life. Maybe such dreams represent a daughter's acknowledgment that there were more sides to the mother than she had been ready to accept. Or maybe she had not noticed her mother had been changing in ways the dream made more evident. Maybe the dream mother was the mother her daughter had always wanted. There are, of course, as many interpretations as there are dreamers.

Some women I spoke with related specific experiences in which they actually felt their mothers' presence. Jean, who had been with her mother up to and including the last minutes, said that the death was "the most real experience of my life." She swears that what happened after the funeral is true. "After my mother died and we returned to the house from the funeral, I saw her face as I was resting on the floor. She was winking at me and I felt she directed me to a drawer I would have otherwise never opened and hidden under some papers was $200." Jean explained that because her father was "so tight with a dollar," her mother was often stashing money away.

Lora also feels she received a special gift from her mother. She was with her mother when she died, and actually felt the soul leave the body. "Right after that I needed to be alone. I went out across the frozen field and kept walking looking for a quiet way to say good-bye to my mother. Then I looked up and there was the slowest shooting star I had ever seen moving across the sky from East to West. I felt it was my mother saying good-bye to me—so we each had a chance to say good-bye." Both stories point to the daughters' feelings that the relationship and even their communication with their mothers had survived their deaths.

Georgia, tough, hard-minded, who said her mother should have had dogs instead of children, said "She's been back. I was in the hospital in ICU in the past year. They wanted to put me on a respirator. I had pneumonia. I was out of it and the room turned ruby red and I knew my mother and grandmother were in a corner of the room. I said to them, 'You have to help me. It is not my time to go. I really need your help to get well,' and there was whispering in the corner and that night I turned the corner and started to get better. So I knew my mother was there."

Terri, strongly attached to her religious faith, said that a week before the Jewish New Year, "I felt the presence of both of my parents. When I was reaching into a drawer, I put my hand on something that gave me a real shock and it turned out to be my mother's measuring spoons."

Koru, who had been living with her mother in an apartment her brother owned, had no idea how she would work things out after her mother died, or even where she would live. She said that shortly after her mother's death, she and her brother and sister-in-law met to decide what to do with the apartment. "We worked together like my mother was telling us what to do and we all said yes."

Some of the expressions mothers used remain, sometimes for the better, sometimes not. Vivian recalled that whenever there was something unsaid or unsettling "my mother would close off the conversation by saying, "That's the way it is." Vivian said she was always unpleasantly surprised to hear those words come out of her own mouth, but she took them as a reminder that her mother was still with her in yet another way.

MOVING AHEAD

Moss found that after the death of a parent, most children, at least middle-aged children, continue their lives much the same as they did when the parent was alive, having already incorporated some values and attitudes of their parents and rejected others [3, p. 109]. If continuity of lifestyle is evidence of mastery of transition, then most people handled the deaths of their mothers quite well. Most of the women I talked to had not and did not anticipate going through major changes. They did, however, recognize some important changes they had made or wanted to make for the future.

It's in the letting go that one finds significant possibilities. Losing parents when already an adult can be a real encouragement to growth according to Judith Viorst [4, p. 295]. It can push daughters (and sons) into becoming self-defining grownups at last, and make possible a new maturity, something out of the reach of women who still saw themselves as so-and-so's daughter. Three months after her mother died, one seventy-five-year-old woman told me, "For the first time in my life, I feel like a grown-up."

Moss characterizes this adjustment as an integral part of the mourning process. He observed that the death of parents may "usher in a sense of needing to reorganize the self as a way to deal with the profound impact of the loss." What is desired, he found, is a "feeling of autonomy that flows from a deep sense of one's identity" [3, p. 111]. This feeling can come out of the willingness to face life as it is or was, and not as one would have liked or wanted it to be.

An aspect of this new maturity often includes reevaluating one's own life and goals, questioning what is important. Irene is one of the daughters who found herself reevaluating her life after her mother died and started doing things differently. Strongly urged by her mother to be successful, Irene obtained a Ph.D. and has always worked very hard. She said, "My life has changed since my mother died. I no longer have the same need to meet all my obligations; I tell myself that if a report is in a little late, it is not the end of the world. I just don't have the same drive to get things done in the same way. I'm not sure this is related to my mother's death, but something about seeing that the only outcome of life is ultimately death makes the day-to-day less important."

Rachel, too, experienced changes in her outlook on the world. "A few months ago I was at a stage where it felt like time was standing still—maybe that is a more active stage of grief, but it is still there and maybe it will always be there. A feeling that my own mortality, my own ending took much more prominence than it ever had. I'm fifty-five and have maybe twenty-five more years. . . . I would like to spend more time on reflection. I have more of an acute awareness of not starting projects I really don't want to do. . . . I'm keenly aware of the need to decide how I'm going to live my life. I'm not afraid of dying but it is scary to think of it ending. I feel an urgency to get some perspective."

What Irene and Rachel felt is not unusual. Kennedy found that trying to figure out how to live when death is so real often leads to a new appreciation of each moment. Moss makes a similar observation, that the loss of a parent forces the child to face death, but also to confront its opposite—life and personal growth. To cope successfully with this death means "neither reifying the past nor leaving it behind but assimilating it as one's psychological inheritance." A daughter can own the positive aspects of the connection in order to become a better parent and member of the family to those remaining in her life. She has the chance to end a conflict-ridden relationship and use that energy more productively. She can challenge uncomfortable restrictions the parents placed on her and can see them in some perspective. In that way, she has the opportunity to generate a "new core of expectations."

One of the major changes Rachel wished to make in her life included "making a different and increased effort not to repeat my mother's mistakes with my own kids." This priority was shared by many who wished to establish a more satisfying relationship and rapport with their own children than they had had with their mothers, both in their mothers' prime and at the end. Annie stated that she wanted to make sure that she never does anything that involves comparing one child to the other, or even criticizing one to the other, both of which her mother did often. She had been estranged from her sister since they were teenagers and felt that her mother's need to play one daughter against the other was one of the primary factors in this conflict.

One's psychological inheritance also has to do with the daughter avoiding aspects of her mother she didn't like. Jorrie said that "on the first holiday after my mother died, I must have unconsciously moved into my mother's place. It became clear when I saw the video. I heard myself sounding just like my mother. I promised I wouldn't become my mother." Patti said she saw how much her mother's snobbishness and critical attitudes cut her off from other people and she wanted to make sure she remained open.

"My mother died with too many things unsaid," was one of Suzanne's major regrets. Feeling frustrated and sad, Suzanne wanted her relationship with her children to be open and honest. "I want to make sure that our relationship is authentic. That we don't waste our time talking about things that don't matter or avoiding the big things out of fear of hurting each other."

MAKING PLANS

Several women used what they learned about themselves and their mothers to start planning ahead. Jorie realized that she doesn't want to make her children responsible for what happens to her, the way her mother did. "I don't want them to have to be the ones who decide what becomes of me. I would like to be in a place where there is the care I need so I won't have to count on them." Marcia, who felt "terribly hurt" that her mother had not left a note or a special possession with her name on it, decided to write a letter to each daughter, telling her how much she loved her and, with the letter, to put a special token, something she knew each girl would want, something that had special significance.

Some of the daughters' resolutions for change have to do with their interactions with others. Sukie realizes more than ever that "I want to live my life as if I might die tomorrow. I want to spend more time doing what I want, rather than what I should. I want to clear up all misunderstandings. I want to make sure that I always let each person I care about know they are a gift in my life." Sukie found out which friends she could count on and those she couldn't while she was taking care of her mother and mourning her death. She doesn't want to spend time with people who are not really friends.

LOOKING AT FAMILY

Several daughters felt a need to reconnect with other family members, an impulse that arose as a result of the death and planning of the funeral. This is not surprising. The period after a parent's death can be a time not only for grief, but for redefining relationships between bereaved survivors, particularly siblings. Siblings who have shared grief and are now parentless often find they need to redefine their relationships with their siblings.

Madeline, who had moved away from home when she married, had had almost no contact with her brother or other family members for more than thirty-five years. Dealing with the funeral and burial arrangements, she and her family reconnected and "for the first time I feel as if I have a brother. I even call some of my aunts and uncles, people I haven't talked to for years." Two years after her mother died, she went back to Greece where her mother was born and had spent the first eighteen years of her life. Madeline met aunts and uncles she had never seen. She was overwhelmed when they showed her the pictures they had saved of her, of how much they were like her mother, and how much more she was able to know about her mother by seeing her life from this new perspective.

There is a brief time right after a parent's death when the family is opened up to change. Kennedy noticed with her clients that this loss of the center opens up all kinds of possibilities. She explains that when faced with the death of a parent, you can either blindly be part of a new system or you can take the initiative and find a new system that is right for you. This means speaking up for what you want, exploring new ways of connecting, and fighting against the old ways that can creep up on you if you are not aware. She observes that many families, at this time, have found it valuable to use some form of therapy to help the family find new and better ways of being together [5, p. 108].

Ruthellen had never really lived with her mother, a foreign missionary whose children were sent home when they were old enough to attend school. Early on, although each sibling had a strong connection to the mother, it was not to the family. Ruthellen said that since their mother's death, the siblings have established closer contact with each other. She and her sister, for the first time, are doing things together.

Elaine also left home when she was young. Though functioning as a mature adult in most areas of her life, she still felt like a child in terms of taking initiative in contacting any family members. She didn't have to be responsible for remembering to drop a card or make a call, she confessed, as long as her mother was around to remind her of her obligations. After her mother's death, however, Elaine didn't want those connections to die with her mother. Even she was surprised, she said, when she started calling these aunts and uncles, and writing to her mother's brother each week, just as her mother had done. And since her mother had always been the go-between for her and her brother, often to the detriment of their relationship, they were now talking to each other directly. Like several others, Elaine lost a mother and found a sibling.

The opposite is also possible. Karen had never gotten along with her brother, feeling he was always disinterested and remote, but had kept up a very superficial relationship with him for her mother's sake. Her mother repeatedly asked her to promise that she and her brother would remain close after she died. Sometimes she would promise, Karen said, and sometimes when she knew her mother could take some teasing, she'd ask her, "What difference will it make to you?" After their mother's death, Karen started questioning whether she even wanted her brother in her life. At the time we talked, she was trying to decide what, if any, kind of relationship she wanted to have with her brother.

Meg wanted to end her relationships with her siblings completely. Her mother's death had been very painful and hard on Meg, who was so grieved to watch her mother slip from the once proud, intellectual family matriarch to a woman who had to be removed from the board-and-care facility because she was attacking other patients. During her mother's decline, Meg felt she received no support or help from her brothers and sister, even though she had as many competing obligations as they. By the time her mother died, she wanted nothing more to do with them. Not only had they let her down, Meg felt they had unforgivably let their mother down. Again, this was not a unique situation.

The death of a parent can be hard on all family members, often weakening the bonds that connect them. The tensions and emotional pain arising from the death can lay bare, or bring about, painful rifts in families. According to one theory, these sibling conflicts and emotional outbursts serve to block out the actual grief and divert attention from the psychological pain of losing a parent. Group or family therapy can be extremely helpful if these conflicts persist and become unmanageable [3, p. 127].

SELECTIVE INTEGRATION

Moss tells us that tough-mindedness seems essential, particularly when evaluating one's relationship with parents. Personal growth does not demand a rejection of parental legacies but rather a *selective integration of them into one's own value system* (emphasis added) [3, p. 111].

From what many have said, this internalizing and identifying with the valued aspects of the mother enrich a daughter and help her to grow in ways she might not have anticipated. In the same way, this internalizing and identifying helps the mourner bridge the generations to make a lasting connection.

Cory found her mother was with her in a way she never foresaw. She said that she is so much more aware of her mother than when her mother was alive that her mother is "closer to me in some spiritual way—I don't think there is a day that goes by that I don't see myself doing something—whether it is slicing vegetables, putting plates back, catching a glimpse of myself in the mirror—saying something, cutting something out of the newspaper—hundreds of gestures that for some reason—it is like my mother is inhabiting my body. I'm not somebody who believes in a lot of unconventional theories—I will look at my hand and I will see my mother's hand. It makes her somewhat more present in my life, in a way mixed with guilt and in a way that alleviates the guilt."

Dori, a remarkably creative artist and writer, also felt her mother's presence in her life. She explained, "My whole thinking life I have been most interested in time versus space, a sense of things being more spacial than chronological. My mother is now present in a different way. When she was alive, when she was well, and when she was sick. I see all those pictures, even what she looked like at sixteen. She is totally present in the atmosphere around me. Shortly after she died, I had a dream that I was at her house, the door bell rang and she was on the other side. I could see her through the lace, through the glass—she had turned into one of her photos."

SUMMING UP

It's a bit disconcerting to think of the loss of one's mother as providing a potential for growth. After all, it was she who played the major role in your growth from the very beginning. In almost every instance, she was the one who taught you to tie a shoe, bake a cake, and cover the earliest signs of graying hair. Now, even in death, she is not through teaching, if you can tune in to the sound of what you hold in your head and in your heart.

You can use her death as a time to make necessary adjustments in your own life, ones you've been putting off. Now you can toss out or incorporate what she was giving you—a target for your anger, a shelter for your vulnerability, a voice of uncritical acceptance, a go-between for you and other family members, or the preserver of childhood memories.

You now have the chance to discard what doesn't serve you and to assimilate that which feeds your spirit. Those who are able to use this time to reconsider what is important, what they want to give to others and receive in return, are giving themselves a wonderful gift. One can see, finally, the significant opportunities that can accompany loss, when one openly acknowledges and grieves. So many women find that the death of their mother carries, along with the sadness, the potential for making oneself stronger, more authentic, more open to love, more committed to what matters, and more accepting of the complexities and wonder of being alive.

It starts with keeping what is important—keepsakes, memories, messages, connections—and letting go of what no longer belongs in your life.

REFERENCES

1. S. de Beauvoir, *A Very Easy Death,* Pantheon Books, New York, 1965.
2. M. A. Robbins, *Midlife Women and Death of Mother: A Study of Psychohistorical and Spiritual Transformation,* Peter Lang, New York, 1990.
3. M. S. Moss and S. Z. Moss, *The Final Transition,* Baywood, Amityville, New York, 1995.
4. J. Viorst, *Necessary Losses: The Love, Illusion, Dependencies and Impossible Expectations that All of Us Have to Give Up in Order to Grow,* Fawcett Gold Metal, New York, 1987.
5. A. Kennedy, *Losing a Parent, Passage to a New Way of Living,* Harper, San Francisco/New York, 1991.

Conclusion

Maybe it's true what they say about our generation—the one born just before and during World War II—that ours will be the one that lets nothing happen without examining it "to death." Yet, it's only through this kind of attention that we can learn from what we experience. Though ironic, it is by talking, probing, questioning, that we are not only able to make important discoveries about ourselves and our mothers, but we prove, once and for all, that we are not our mothers, with their need for secrecy, or their reticence and reluctance to talk about painful things. We are doing the antithesis of what our mothers would have done.

As the first wave of daughters this side of the divide, we have seen and done things differently than our mothers, both in the ways we live our lives, and in the way we create our relationships. We pass on our generational insights and lessons to our children who, in their turn, will also choose and learn differently than we.

The impetus for this book was both personal and seemingly straightforward—I wanted to better understand my own reactions to my mother's death and to learn from other women who had recently experienced the same loss. I wanted to know what it meant that I didn't fall apart when others I knew did. What did that say about me? About them? I also wanted to know about those women who felt great freedom when their mother died; what did they know that left them not sad, but relieved? These questions, of course, led to the bigger ones—what made the loss harder for some women than others? I even hoped to discover what kind of relationships were easier to let go. I wanted equations and was naive enough to think I might get them.

I also found that despite the silence I initially encountered, other daughters wanted to talk about this experience, too. Their stories reveal that this death affected most of them deeply, and with it they mourned the loss of many things of value: not only the chance to talk and be with their mothers, to stay connected, but those lucky enough to have seen in their mothers "their best cheerleader" would miss the opportunity to ever again be on the receiving end of such unconditional love. Most daughters acknowledged that with the deaths of their mothers they had lost their roots, much of their history, and the illusion they still had time before their own lives ended.

RANGE OF RESPONSES

In looking back at the stories, I am surprised at the range of responses among the women I interviewed: how positive some were, and how negative others. I had not anticipated the experiences of some women who talked about how grateful they felt to have the chance to be with their mothers as they were dying. They used words like "blessed," "fortunate," and "honored." They did not blame their mothers (or themselves) for past failures, did not mention adolescent fights, or the need to distance themselves. Their consciences were clear. These women seemed to have particularly honest relationships with their mothers. They just seemed large—the daughters as well as the dying mothers. They appreciated each other.

I was also surprised by the other extreme: the women who expressed not a shred of sorrow at their mothers' deaths. These daughters had experienced what they considered to be abusive relationships, and they were very ready to shed the baggage of filial obligations and keep going. They had no kind words for their mothers, remembering clearly all they disliked, the betrayals and grievances, even those that had occurred more than forty years earlier. For most of the women, however, their responses fell somewhere in between the two.

As a reader, you will have no doubt recognized among these daughters those who have shared experiences similar to yours, and perhaps you have been reassured by the knowledge that you are not alone. And above all, these stories serve to remind us how significant is the mother-daughter bond and how important it is to redefine that bond for ourselves, even now, after our mothers have died. And certainly, those of us with daughters of our own have an opportunity to reexamine that bond as well.

After personally interviewing more than forty-five women and reviewing the significant research on women, age, and loss, I found that, ultimately, three factors seem to bear on the way daughters dealt with their mothers' death: the mother herself; the personality of the daughter; and the kind of relationship the two shared. Of course, as the stories illustrated, none of these factors stands alone; each influences the others. So the challenge for us is to unravel these threads and trace them back to their beginning, if we are to gain an understanding of our mothers, ourselves, and the legacies they left and we'll leave to future generations.

MOTHERS AND DAUGHTERS

The relationship of mother and daughter started with the unique individual each was, deep down in her DNA structure, and then developed through the interplay of personalities and the socio-historic circumstances of their lives. Drawing from the examples of the women I talked with, it seems apparent that the most loving and comfortable relationships started with a mother who found a way to be nurturing and positive, no matter the circumstances, and communicate this to her daughter. Unfortunately, this was not always easy, or perhaps even possible for many of the women whose daughters I interviewed.

Because of the times in which they were born and grew up, many of our mothers were often weighed down with deep sadness and/or anger. Many, too, if not subjected to hardship, never had the choices and options their daughters enjoyed; still other mothers, because of their own isolation and/or lack of self-esteem, were overly dependent on their daughters for sympathy, friendship, and companionship. But those mothers who had been even modestly independent, loving, and nurturing, either because they had been able to put the pain and disappointment of their own lives behind them, or had lived more blessed lives (or been more accepting of the lives they had), enjoyed the most companionship and help from their daughters during and at the end of their lives.

Those daughters who did not grow up steeped in their mothers' misery or anger, did not feel responsible for making everything all right for them, or smothered by their mothers' dependence on them were able to have a relationship that at its core was based on mutual respect. These women seemed most able to authentically grieve their loss, and then, with the warmest of memories, gain the perspective to get on with their lives.

By contrast, those who felt burdened, demeaned, or ignored by their mothers took one of two courses. Some—whose mothers were angry, depressed, jealous, or just plain difficult—found ways by which they could come to terms with their mothers and so were able to grieve their death and move on with their lives without too much disruption. For some, this meant taking a time-out from the relationship, usually in early adulthood, before reengaging with their mothers in a less conflicted way. Sometimes they turned to therapy or other activities that gave them a new perspective. Others benefitted from the passage of time. But regardless of how they got there, these daughters, too, were able to be supportive of their mothers as they were dying. They learned to see their mothers in their historical context, in order to understand the world in which their mothers lived and, at least to some degree, understand the forces that made their mothers the way they were. Understanding led to acceptance and often forgiveness.

Those daughters who had difficult mothers and took no such steps—gaining distance or seeking professional help—were often unfazed or even relieved when their mothers died. One cannot predict how they will come to terms with this loss over time. And still others, who took the full brunt of their mothers' bitterness and suffering, blamed themselves for not being able to relieve it, and often struggled terribly at their mothers' deaths with unresolved issues of guilt and grief.

Finally, there were the relationships in which mother and daughter seemed never to become too entwined. Gena had great regard for her mother, moved away not out of anger but due to her husband's career, and never seemed to have had a need for anything closer than casual phone calls and good wishes. This kind of relationship seemed to develop in those situations where the mothers were not dependent on their daughter for emotional or practical support. The daughters grew up to be independent and loving women; they did their best to be at the side of their dying mothers, grieved their passing, and got on with their lives.

By midlife, different factors often arose to influence the relationship, including other losses the daughters had to contend with. In some cases, these losses seemed to diminish the importance of their mother's life and death, while for others it seemed to intensify the relationship. In these cases, much seems to depend on the kind of support the mothers were able to give their daughters. Joan felt even closer to her mother because of the way her mother had comforted and supported her when her son died. But Nancy felt even more distant when she realized that her mother had nothing to give her when her daughter died. Several of the women were widows but, again, the deaths of their husbands brought them either closer to or farther away from their mothers, depending on how helpful their mothers were. Usually, there were no surprises. Most of these daughters say they could have predicted how their mothers would respond during times of loss.

LESSONS LEARNED

We had no choice as to the families into which we were born, nor the historical circumstances in which our lives and our mothers' took place. It may seem, also, that once our mothers are dead, there is nothing more for us to do about this relationship but close the door. In many important ways, however, a mother's death is only the beginning of a new phase in the mother-daughter relationship, a defining period at that.

As I mined these stories for their common threads and unique insights, I looked for lessons that would help others like myself prepare for and heal from this turning point, the death of one's mother. I was struck by how valuable the women I interviewed found the opportunity to talk about their mothers' lives and deaths, as if there were so much at stake in understanding and coming to terms with their mother, their relationship, and themselves.

From this arose a major discovery, one I was not even looking for. I began to see how much potential we have in the wake of our mothers' deaths to change not only our own lives for the future, but our mothers' legacies as well. So what did I find for the handbook on ways to deal with our mother's death? Here are some of the lessons that come through loud and clear.

It's important that we grieve authentically—for our mother, for our own sake, and for the sake of our legacy. Love her or not, she's been in your life for more than five decades. If you can't allow yourself to grieve what is lost, something remains frozen and you may compromise your ability to live the rest of your life with authenticity.

Take note of your feelings, perhaps by writing them down, perhaps by talking about them with a friend. Don't worry if they're "crazy" or contradictory; this is true for just about everyone. What is it you have lost? What is it you grieve? Name the little things you'll miss, as well as the large. Realize that you grieve for yourself as well as your mother.

By this time, it should be possible to disengage from our earliest feelings about our mothers and formulate new, more mature ones, ones that take into account the realities of their own lives and how those realities affected their ability to be our mothers. As mature adults, we should be able to recognize and accommodate all dimensions of our mothers. We know it is not realistic nor does it serve us or our mothers to canonize or demonize them. To our earlier understandings we can add our own experiences as adults and perhaps parents, and use this lens to view our mothers' efforts.

We learn from the women who had the opportunity to say good-bye to their mothers in a meaningful way that we have the responsibility to understand the relationship we have had with our mother, over all the phases of our lives, and to make peace with what it was and is. It is in coming to terms that we can free ourselves from the conflicts. And unless we do free ourselves, it is possible that these conflicts will continue to play themselves out with other significant people in our lives.

We also get a chance to see how important it is for our own development (which doesn't stop until our deaths) to sift through the enormous complexity of feelings this death triggered. If there is guilt, we need to recognize this. Guilt is often a convenient mask for other feelings, and it is worth looking through it to see what lies beneath it. Guilt serves no purpose; it interferes with our memory of our mother, shortchanges us, and robs those who love us. The sorrow, loss, and the relief, all these feelings must be experienced as well, for it is only by experiencing and examining them that we can gain some closure on this very large chapter in our lives.

Grief takes its own time and its own direction. To go through this process and come out the other side, it is necessary to acknowledge (even though others may not) the significance of this loss. Given the strength of most mother-daughter relationships, this loss can take its toll in many ways: emotionally, physically, and cognitively. It is important that we give ourselves the care we need, whether it is for a month or a year.

MOVING ON

In the years that have passed since I began this study, I continue to explore this phenomenon of my mother's death and its effect on my life. One day I find myself irritated by some silly remark she made a decade ago, and another time I find myself overwhelmed with gratitude for what she did for me. Yesterday I heard a voice in the back of my head say to me, "You're worrying too much about nothing. You can't please everyone." Maybe it was her speaking. Maybe it was me. At this point, I have come to recognize her influence and my acceptance of it in so many ways.

She is still alive for me. I still find reasons to get mad and reasons to honor her. The former is diminishing, the latter is not. I knew I had moved through grief when I so strongly connected with what she did for me and how well it serves me:

BLOOMING

Four years after her death
my mother's violets bloom
tyrannically. She had two green thumbs,
I've none. Yet each day new buds burst
through old leaves—always plumping
themselves up—fat and succulent
like pillows whipped up
by good mothers

Maybe it's what she did for them,
new that summer—
leaching egg shells in water for calcium,
turning them to the sun's angle

In the same way, it must be
what she did for me—
forgiving that tyrant who refused her breast,
tickling, teasing out a smile

I have to believe in first moves—otherwise
how would I know about filling empty hands,
what belongs in the crook of a neck,
how to find the one story
to make my desperately ill daughter laugh
when I really wanted

to be hiding or dying or
swimming the English Channel

It must be all in those first
shallow breaths that we get it right;
from then it all keeps
tumbling over and after.

                              Diane Sher Lutovich

Suggested Reading

Ainley, Rosa (ed.), *Death of a Mother: Daughters' Stories,* Pandora, London, 1994.

Akner, Lois F., *How to Survive the Loss of a Parent: A Guide for Adults,* William Morrow and Co., New York, 1993.

Brooks, Jane, *Midlife Orphan: Facing Life's Changes Now That Your Parents Are Gone,* Berkley Publishing Group, New York, 1999.

Curry, Cathleen L., *When Your Parent Dies,* Ave Maria Press, Notre Dame, Indiana, 1993.

Edelman, Hope, *Motherless Daughters: The Legacy of Loss,* Dell, New York, 1994.

Friday, Nancy, *My Mother My Self: The Daughter's Search for Identity,* Delacorte Press, New York, 1977.

Levine, Stephen, *Meetings At the Edge: Dialogues with the Grieving and the Dying, the Healing and the Healed,* Anchor Books, New York, 1984.

Marshall, Fiona, *Losing a Parent,* Fisher Books, Tucson, Arizona, 1993.

Myers, Edward, *When Parents Die,* Penguin Books, New York, 1986.

Rando, Therese A., *How to Go On Living When Someone You Love Dies,* Bantam Books, New York, 1991.

Schiff, Harriet Sarnoff, *Living Through Mourning: Finding Comfort and Hope When a Loved One Has Died,* Viking, New York, 1987.

Index